"*Honoring Dishonorable Pastage of life who want to parents but are struggling with what it looks like and how it is to be lived out in their specific situation."

Patsy Clairmont, Author of *Twirl…A Fresh Spin at Life*

"Jan Frank has written a much needed book on what it means to honor your parents especially when your parents have behaved dishonorably towards you. Even as a Christian counselor, I struggled with how I would fulfill this command with my own abusive mother, without feeling like I was pretending or placating. Jan gives us that *how to*; masterfully combining biblical truth and grace."

Leslie Vernick, licensed counselor, relationship coach, speaker and the author of *The Emotionally Destructive Marriage* and *The Emotionally Destructive Relationship*

"Jan Frank's latest book, *Honoring Dishonorable Parents* does what her other books have done so well—it speaks frankly, biblically and practically about some of life's deepest pains. When we suffer at the hands of our parents or are neglected at the hands of our parents or abandoned by them entirely, how do we respond in any positive way, let alone with forgiveness and grace? Speaking from her own life, Jan Frank leads us through processes of restoration and reconciliation, both with God and potentially with those less-than-honorable parents. This is a book which will communicate comfort and hope to so many who desperately need both."

Jenni Key, Director of Women's Ministries, First Evangelical Free Church, Fullerton, CA

"Jan Frank tackles a sensitive issue that is faced by many adult children with extreme tenderness and sound teaching. Jan's passion comes from her personal understanding of the issue plus her experience as a family therapist and counselor. I recommend this book to anyone who wants to understand how to honor dishonorable parents or who are helping with people who suffer from the pain and anxiety of this issue. Thank you, Jan, for a well done and timely book that will give so many practical help and biblical hope."

    Wayne Hastings, Author of *The Way Back from Loss* and Resources Pastor, Grace Chapel, Leipers Fork, TN

"*Honoring Dishonorable Parents*" addresses a critical topic in today's fractured world. Much confusion exists around the biblical commands to honor one's parents and Jan Frank addresses these issues with compassion, insight, and strength. Jan's own story gives her wisdom, depth, and empathy. This is a very important book and one that should be read by many."

    Mike Erre, Senior Pastor, First Evangelical Free Church Fullerton, CA and author of *Astonished: Recapturing the Wonder, Awe, and Mystery of Life with God*

"With warmth and wisdom, courageous transparency and down-to-earth candor, Jan Frank puts the practical "how to" alongside the biblical "thou shalt" of honoring our parents. This book will be read by many with a deep sigh and a whispered prayer of thanksgiving for a sister who truly understands and a Father who truly cares."

    Scott E. Wigginton, Ph.D., LMFT, Professor at Campbellsville University, Counseling Pastor, Campbellsville Baptist Church

"We have known Jan Frank since she was a young adult and have witnessed her journey of healing and restoration from early childhood pain. Throughout her journey, her diligence and deep desire to follow God and His will for her life have been paramount. In many ways, *Honoring Dishonorable Parents* is a culmination of her journey coupled with her experience as a counselor. In it she provides practical guidelines for those who want to know how to maintain respectful, caring behavior towards their parents, in a healthy, God-honoring way. We highly endorse this book for those who've struggled with what it looks like to honor parents who've acted in *"less than honorable ways."*

> Bob and Emilie Barnes, *co-founders of More Hours in My Day Ministries*

"Jan Frank has given to her readers a precious gift in her book, *Honoring Dishonorable Parents*. Interwoven with the narratives of her own life and others', this book reverberates with insight, offering life and hope for those whose lives have been marked by wounds inflicted by their parents. Grounded in biblical truth, framed by inter-personal wisdom, and steeped in divine grace, *Honoring Dishonorable Parents* invites readers to come to terms with their own painful histories, while it summons them forward into new stages of healing. Frank not only affirms, but she personally demonstrates that the counterintuitive pathway to wholeness runs through graciously forgiving and relinquishing the very ones who failed us in the tender years."

> Jonathon Lunde PhD, associate professor of biblical and theological studies at Talbot School of Theology, Biola University and author of *Following Jesus, the Servant King: A Biblical Theology of Covenantal Discipleship*

HONORING
Dishonorable
PARENTS

**Helping Heal and Restore
Family Relationships**

Unless otherwise noted, Scripture quotations are from the Holy Bible, New Living Translation, copyright ©1996, 2004, 2007 by Tyndale House Foundation. Used by permission of Tyndale House Publishers, Inc., Carol Stream, Illinois 60188. All rights reserved.

Scripture quotations marked (NIV) are from the Holy Bible, New International Version, Copyright © 1973, 1978, 1984, 2011 by Biblica, Inc. Used by permission. All rights reserved worldwide.

Scripture quotations marked (NKJV) are from the New King James Version. Copyright © 1982 by Thomas Nelson, Inc. Used by permission. All rights reserved.

ISBN 978-1-50327-302-3

© 2014 Grace Chapel

No part of this book may be reproduced or transmitted without the expressed written permission of the publisher. This includes all types of means including photocopying, recording or electronic media. Please direct your inquiries for permission and bulk sales to: wayne@gracechapel.net

Grace Chapel
3279 Southall Road
Leipers Fork, TN 37064

To follow Jan's blog or inquire about speaking engagements please contact her through her web-site: Contact info: www.janfrank.org

HONORING Dishonorable PARENTS

Helping Heal and Restore
Family Relationships

JAN FRANK, MFT

To Dotty, my "spiritual mother"

WORDS OF THANKS

I am indebted to my dear friend and intercessor, Jenni Key, whose encouraging words over lunch were the catalyst that started me writing. Thank you for the hours you spent reading and re-reading the manuscript, offering your editing expertise, and clarity of thought. Thanks also for generously providing a lovely place to write—your beach cottage was a blessing!

To the women in my Pursuit Bible study who graciously offered their encouragement, prayer, and support as I stepped away from my duties to follow God's direction of writing this book. A special thanks to my teaching team who filled the gap and prayed me through from beginning to end: Cathy Redmond, Katie Smylie, Jenn Hale, Gwen Botka, and Katie Potesta. You're the best! And, to my sweet friend Stephanee whose prayers move me.

To Laurinda, whose on-going personal journey was the impetus to keep me writing. To the many clients, friends, and survey respondents who shared their stories. All stories have been altered or blended in order to protect your confidentiality. Thank you for enriching this book through your sincere desire to know what it looks like to honor dishonorable parents.

To my life-time prayer warriors and friends: Dotty, Marian, Ginny, Emilie, Heidi and Kim. You've been beside me along much of this journey and always provided godly wisdom, counsel, and insight. Thank you!

To my friend and mentor, Wayne Hastings who championed this book from the moment he heard about it. Thank you, Wayne for challenging me to be better than I am in so many areas! Your vast publishing knowledge is only surpassed by your humility and love for our Savior. Thank you to Dan Marrs, my editor whose keen insight, comments, and logical thought process contributed immensely to sharpening this book and making it better. I appreciate you so much! Thank you to Bart Dawson for his cover concept and design.

To my sweetheart and husband of thirty-five years, Don. Thank you for embracing my calling, often at your own expense. You have partnered with me through this process many times before, always without a word of complaint. You are God's greatest gift to me as we walk this pilgrimage together. I'm so thankful to be on "the ancient path" with you. You're my hero! To our beautiful daughters, Heather and Kellie—may the fruit of this work blossom in your lives and the lives of your children.

Above all, my deepest gratitude goes to my One and Only true Father, whose love and faithfulness continue to transform and sustain me. Thank you, LORD for rescuing and redeeming that lost little girl so long ago. My heart will forever be full of praise and thankfulness for your grace and mercy!

TABLE OF CONTENTS

Preface	13
Introduction	15

Section I: What Honor Doesn't Mean — 23

1. Honoring Doesn't Mean Pleasing — 29
2. Honoring Doesn't Mean Pretending — 43
3. Honoring Doesn't Mean Subjecting Yourself or Your Children to Harm — 50
4. Honoring Doesn't Mean Becoming Entangled in Unhealthy Relational Patterns — 62
5. Honoring Doesn't Mean Being Overly-Responsible — 75
6. Honoring Doesn't Mean Ignoring Illegal, Immoral, or Toxic Behavior — 86

Section II: What Honor Means — 101

7. Honor: What the Bible Teaches — 103
8. Honor: What Jesus' Life Teaches — 117

Section III: Honor Lived Out in Adulthood — 133

9. Show Kindness and Respect — 136
10. Speak the Truth in Love — 141
11. Set a Pattern of Loving Behavior — 148
12. Seek to Settle Issues — 155
13. Submit to God's Authority and Sovereignty — 159

Section IV: The Blessings of Honor   168
14. The Blessing of Relinquishment   171
15. The Blessing of Peace   183
16. The Blessing of Giving Grace   187
17. The Blessings of Obedience   189

An Invitation: Honor in Your Life   192
Epilogue   194
Endnotes   198
Bibliography   205

PREFACE

Honoring Dishonorable Parents is the fruit of my life story; I just didn't know it until recently.

I spent twenty years as a Marriage/Family Therapist listening to people share about their family background and what it was like to grow up in their home. I heard stories that were both heartwarming and heartbreaking. From some, I heard about sweet memories of bedtime stories, ball games and Barbie dolls. From others, I heard about bedlam created by alcoholism, nonstop belittling, and prolonged battles between divorced parents over custody and visitation rights. Many of my clients could still recall those traumatic events with uncanny vividness, even years later. As I listened, I could identify with the loss and disappointment that resulted from growing up with *dishonorable* parents.

A few years ago, my husband Don and I had the privilege of being mentors in a young marrieds class at our church. Most of the couples were in the very first few years of marriage and were adjusting to each other and each other's families. We had the opportunity to share some things we'd learned from our own experiences and to hear the struggles that many of these young couples faced daily.

Surprisingly, both my former clients and these young married couples had something in common: they were trying to figure out how to relate to their parents, even though all of them were now well into adulthood. Many expressed a genuine desire to honor their parents as outlined in the Ten Commandments but wondered what that would look like in their specific situation.

Through the years of my practice and this mentoring experience, I realized that there was very little written about *what it looks like* to honor parents who have lived less than honorably. I realized in talking with men and women at various life stages that many of them held themselves to an idealized and often "unhealthy" concept of what it meant to "honor your father and mother" (Exodus 20:12; Deuteronomy 5:16). Furthermore, while many had some notion of what honor is, very few had been taught what honor *isn't*.

I resonated with them. As a teenager committed to following Jesus and well into my adulthood, I struggled with understanding and living out what it means to honor my parents. I earnestly wanted to honor them because I loved God and desired to be obedient to His Word. There were just a few troubling questions that I couldn't escape: How do I *honor* my parents when they've acted so *dishonorably* toward me? Does God expect me to pretend that the things that went on in our home never happened? Does honoring them involve subjecting my children to some of the very hurtful and sinful actions I experienced as a child?

In this book, I weave the answers to these questions throughout my own story and the stories of others with whom I have walked; most importantly, I answer these questions upon a foundation of Scripture's teachings about what *honor* means and how it is to be lived out.

You will hear the voice of the Bible teacher in me who invites you to grapple with the truths presented in God's Word and exemplified in the life of Jesus as they relate to your life and relationships. You will also hear the voice of the therapist in me whose pragmatism and straightforward approach will offer insight and down-to-earth tools to equip you to deal with *less-than-honorable* parents and other family members. Finally, you will hear the voice of the child in me whose vulnerability and deep longings for connection could not be assuaged without the gentle graciousness of God's indwelling Spirit who is ever at work transforming my heart.

INTRODUCTION

Am I exempt from this command?

I hung up the phone stunned. The conversation I had just had with my eighty-two-year-old mother left me speechless. How, after all these years, could she be so thoughtless?

My stepfather passed away six years ago and since my mother's near-death from cancer four years ago, I have made it a nightly practice to phone her. She lives alone in a modest mobile home in the city where I was born. Our conversations are predictable. She tells me about her day: where she went, what bargains she found at the grocery store, and what she made herself for dinner. We laugh a little, usually about her encounters with people during the day, or we discuss how much money is in the bingo pot primed for a new winner on Monday night in her mobile home park. Occasionally we talk about what is on TV or what book she's currently reading.

Last night was different.

"Hi, mom," I said cheerfully. "How was your day?"

"I'm famous," she told me proudly.

"Oh really," I said, "how so?"

"I got my name in the paper. I wrote a letter to the editor and it got printed."

"Wow, so what did you write about?"

"The city council meetings."

When there's nothing on TV, my mother sits and watches the recorded city council meetings to check up on what is going on around town. Since she's lived in the area for over fifty two years, she is a woman in the know. She knows many of the city's leaders and has worked in her local polling district for years. She has definite ideas about how the city should run and who should run it. She hosted a coffee a couple years ago for her preferred mayoral candidate and was very disappointed when he lost the election. She has no use for the current mayor.

"Why don't you read me what you wrote?"

My mother proceeded to read her letter to the editor. In the midst of a litany of complaints and suggestions for reform, she zinged the mayor for his recent hiring of someone whom he'd failed to "check out"—a vague indictment that piqued my curiosity.

When she finished reading the letter, I asked, "So, Mom, what was that hiring thing about?"

"Well, it was quite the story. Our mayor hired one of his cronies and we later found out he was a child molester."

"How did you find out about it? When did this happen?" I asked.

"Oh, it was a big scandal in the paper a few months ago. I don't know how they found out, but the man they put in charge of this city program for children was a child molester," she said curtly.

"Was he a registered sex offender?" I asked, wanting more clarification.

"Yes," she said, and then added indignantly, "The mayor hired him and didn't even check him out."

You might be wondering why this conversation left me speechless. Why did my mother's legitimate concern for the safety of her community cause me such consternation? In order to understand, you need to know my story.

A Devastated Foundation

I was the youngest of three girls born to my mother and biological father whose marriage ended in divorce after fifteen years. I was five years old when they separated. I still remember the day my biological father packed his bags and left. I followed him to the car with tears streaming down my face, begging my daddy not to leave. I remember saying to myself, "If you're a good enough little girl, daddy will come back." I was never good enough.

After my parents split, my mother became the sole provider. Shortly thereafter, she began dating. She was in her early thirties at this time and was a very attractive woman. In 1963, she married a man named James. I was eight years old. There were lots of changes in our lives as a result. My oldest sister got pregnant and left our home just prior to my mother's marriage to James. I was seven when she left. Her departure ended our relationship, and due to my biological father's sketchy child support payments and my mother and James' disdain for him, my relationship ended with him as well. Our family diminished to my other sister, my mom and stepfather, and me. That is, until my half brother Jimmy was born in early 1964. After being "the baby" of the family for over nine years, I had a replacement.

We moved from our apartment to a nice three-bedroom home in a neighboring city. One of the best changes was that my mother was now a full-time homemaker. This was quite a change, as she had worked outside of the home from the time I was six weeks old.

Another significant change was our church affiliation. As a result of my stepfather's influence, we began regularly attending church. Our church emphasized Scripture memorization, rewarding those children who could recite portions of Scripture, hymns of the faith, and the books of the Bible. Having received little affirmation in my home growing up, I felt I had found my niche. I was memorizing large portions of Scripture, out-performing my peers who'd been in church all their lives and getting the recognition I longed for. Things seemed to be looking up. Despite the brokenness caused by the divorce, I had a new father, a new home, and a new sense of belonging. But I didn't know that two more irreversible life changes were on the horizon.

The Duality of Joy and Sorrow

One January evening, my sister and I went to church by ourselves. A visiting evangelist shared the gospel message and I felt a tug on my heart to respond to his invitation to know Jesus personally. That night, January 17, 1965, at the age of ten, I raised my hand indicating that I had asked Jesus Christ into my heart to be my Savior. I believed with all my heart what the preacher had said: that "God so loved the world that He gave his only Son to die on a cross and pay the penalty for my sin" and that by trusting in Jesus and what he'd done for me, I would be saved and go to heaven.

After the service, we were urged to go to the prayer room. I'll never forget sitting in that room with a very enthusiastic older woman whose joy over my decision could hardly be contained. She sat with me and told me that there were "angels rejoicing in heaven" over me and the decision I'd made. Something happened because the joy she expressed began to pour into my young little heart and I felt more wanted and loved than I had ever felt in my whole life. That was a life-changing event, not only for this life but also for eternity.

Three weeks later, another, very different life-changing event occurred. My mother and sister were at a mother-daughter tea at our church. My stepfather was at home babysitting my brother and me. That night, under the pretense of inviting me to watch television with him, he called me out of my bedroom and sexually abused me.

A month later, my mother asked if anything had happened with my stepfather. I didn't know at the time that my older sister was also being abused. I told my mother what had happened, but never heard another word about it. Life just went on. We continued attending church, sitting in the pew Sunday after Sunday, looking like a normal Christian family. My stepfather served on the board of our church's building project while he destroyed the foundations at home. The abuse continued extensively with my sister until she moved out at eighteen. The abuse continued with me in both overt and covert forms until I moved out of my house at the age of twenty one. My sister and I did not learn of each other's abuse until several years later.

At ten years old, I didn't fully understand the ramifications of either event. I just knew the great joy of being introduced to a Heavenly Father who loved me was gravely overshadowed by the betrayal of my earthly father who was supposed to love me, and the sorrow over a mother who failed to protect me.

You Will Know the Truth . . .

I buried those events deep inside, but at the age of twenty seven they began to resurrect themselves in my daily life in the form of depression, migraine headaches, anger and a critical spirit. I didn't know what was at the root of these emotional issues, but in my devotions one morning, I came across a verse that changed my life: "Behold, You desire truth in the inward parts, and in the hidden part You will make me to know wisdom" (Psalm 51:6 NKJV).

I had not really given the abuse in my past any significant thought for years. I thought I had thoroughly forgiven and moved on. In the days that followed, the Lord impressed upon me that He wanted to heal me—but this could only happen if I faced the truth of what happened and walked the process of healing with Him. I detail that process in my book, *Door of Hope.*

Through the process, God made it clear to me that I needed to talk with my parents about the abuse. With godly professional counsel and God's leading I addressed the issues with my parents. It was a difficult conversation, but I knew God wanted these issues brought into the light. God was at work in their hearts and in mine. As a result of that conversation, my stepfather admitted for the first time what he'd done two decades earlier. Thus began the long road toward reconciliation and restoration. It hasn't been an easy road. It has involved setting up new boundaries for the sake of protecting my children, leveling walls of pretense, opening up new communication patterns, and extending forgiveness.

We have been walking that road of reconciliation and restoration for over twenty years. Much of what I have learned about *honoring dishonorable parents* is a result of this journey. I have not done it perfectly. In fact, I have wrestled with God through much of the process and I've been humbled like Jacob, whose battle with God left him limping but keenly aware of having encountered God face to face.

And there are still times when the wounds of the past are reopened unexpectedly, such as when my mother told me about the letter she'd written to the editor about the mayor hiring a child molester. At times, her insensitivity and lack of compassion left me speechless—it was as if, the past hadn't even happened.

I share my story with you because I know what it is like to be caught in the tension between the devastation of abuse and betrayal at the hands of those whose job it was to love, protect, and nurture me as a child—and the command of God to "honor your father and mother." There are no caveats, no exceptions to this *command for life*.

An Invitation for Life

Through this book, I'm inviting you into my life and the lives of many others who have agonized over what it means to honor parents who've acted dishonorably toward them. The book is divided into four sections, each beginning with a short introductory story that sets the stage.

What honoring your parents doesn't mean answers such questions as:

- Do I have to please my parents when making decisions as an adult?
- Am I dishonoring my parents by talking about what happened in our home growing up?
- Am I obligated to make sure my children have a close relationship with my parents?
- Am I dishonoring my parents if I don't attend every family gathering?
- Am I dishonoring my parents by setting boundaries for the protection of my children?
- How do I *not* get entangled in the ongoing drama between my parents and other siblings?

What honoring your parents does mean addresses the biblical foundation for the fifth commandment through a conversational interview with two scholars. You're invited to take a close look at four snapshots from the life of Jesus and His interactions with His parents and family—snapshots which yield some surprising insights and applicable truths.

How honor is lived out in adulthood looks at five biblically based principles that are exemplified through both my story and the stories of others who are navigating the difficult task of honoring their own *dishonorable* parents.

And finally, you'll walk with me as I unfold the *blessings of honor* I discovered along my own arduous journey, and the hope and freedom that can come as you walk out your journey one step at a time.

My prayer is that you will join me on the journey of exploring what "honoring your parents" *really* means—in this day and age of fractured families and suspicion of authority, and, more especially, in your concrete situation. You will come to realize, as I did, that when you *honor your mother and father,* you honor God and *you* receive the blessing.

SECTION I

WHAT HONOR DOESN'T MEAN

In the last several years I have had numerous conversations with people about what it means to "honor your father and mother." I've been somewhat surprised that most people can give a fairly accurate definition of honor. But it's usually what *follows* their definition that is most telling.

Eva and I were talking over lunch one day after Bible study. I didn't know her well at the time, so we were talking about our families, kids, and where we were in life at that particular time. When I told her I was writing a book about *honoring dishonorable parents,* her eyebrows shot up and she said, "I could use a copy of that right now!" I was surprised by her response so I asked, "What's going on?"

Eva explained that she grew up as a PK (preacher's kid) and although there were some good things about her family life, she'd spent a lot of time and money in counseling trying to sort out the unhealthy aspects of her relationship with her parents.

"My older brother molested me when we were kids," she said. "Mom and Dad dealt with it severely—punishing us both and requiring us to pray and ask God's forgiveness. We were told never to bring it up again. In my family, honoring meant we weren't to answer back, raise our voices, or drag family 'stuff' into public view. And we were to protect my parents' reputation at all costs."

"Are your parents still living?" I asked.

"My mother is, but my father is deceased. It's taken me a long time to come to terms with my relationship with my parents. A few years ago, I was able to bring up the issue of the molestation with them. They couldn't understand why I was 'digging up the past.' After carrying around the shame and having two failed marriages, it was time for me to address our family's issues. My parents were not very supportive and when I wrote them a letter about the impact of my brother's actions and their lack of protection there was little response other than my mother's admonishment to 'forgive' my brother because 'he's been through so much.'"

"That must have been so hard to hear after all those years. Did they ever acknowledge any responsibility for mishandling the situation?" I asked.

"No, but I finally reached a point when I said to myself, *I've done my part, they've responded the only way they know how and I choose to accept them for who they are with their mistakes and imperfections, whether or not they can say what I need to hear. I choose to love them and honor them.* What's difficult for me now is figuring out what it will look like to honor my parents once they've both passed on. I've been asked on a few occasions to share my testimony of the healing God's done in my heart, but I'm wondering if this is in conflict with honoring my parents. I don't think my parents would ever approve of me sharing things about our family. Am I dishonoring them by telling my story?"

I could certainly identify with Eva's question. There was no doubt in my mind that Eva had worked through a lot of her disappointment and grief before coming to that place. It was evident on her face that she was at peace and was genuine in her desire to honor her parents.

What would you say to Eva? Would she be dishonoring her parents by sharing her story? What would you say to me? Am I dishonoring my parents by writing this book? Maybe you can identify with Eva's and my dilemma. You may not have experienced abuse, but you may have struggled with what honoring is—and isn't.

In the early stages of writing this book, I designed an online survey entitled "Honoring your father and mother." There were five basic questions on the survey:

- What does it mean to "honor your father and your mother"?
- What are some specific cultural mandates you were taught regarding honoring your parents?
- As an adult, have you faced any dilemma or confusion concerning what it means to "honor your parents?" How?
- Are there any questions you have about what it means to "honor your father and your mother?" What are they?
- What, if any, challenges do you struggle with in following this command?

Many who responded to the question about what honoring means said things like: "Treat them with respect." "Defer to them, respect them, ask their opinion, be polite, and stay in touch with them." "Speak kindly of them to others and include them when possible." "Take care of them as they age."

Those same respondents expressed confusion in later questions. They agonized over how honor was to be lived out in their own specific situation. Here are some of their comments and questions:

"With a self-absorbed mother and alcoholic father, I have often felt that they have dishonored themselves, the family, and me. So, how could

I possibly honor them? If I feel resentment but try to be kind and caring is that honoring at all?"

"Is it okay to honor them for their position without condoning what they did? How can we separate their actions from their position?"

"What does it look like to honor a parent that is generally dishonorable? Is cutting off all ties with them ever an honorable thing to do?"

"How does honoring fit with being abused? I know that I should honor them, but I was not honored as a child."

"My dad did me wrong growing up and I am just now dealing with it. I have a hard time being angry and feeling it because that would not be honoring of him. But I am not able to move on either."

"As an adult I still honor and respect my parents. I am forty four and still very much want them to be pleased with me. Sometimes, I find myself making decisions based on not wanting to disappoint my parents."

As you can see, most of the respondents have a desire to follow the fifth commandment, but they're unsure as to what that looks like in their specific situation.

In this section, we will specifically focus on *what honor doesn't mean*. You may be wondering why I'm writing about what it doesn't mean before writing about what it does mean. I think for many people the concept of honor has been either idealized or distorted. They think they must always do what pleases their parents, or they have been taught that honoring means you never disagree or voice your opinion. Many who took the survey expressed genuine confusion about what honor is really supposed to look like.

Do you share their confusion? Can you define "honor" while remaining unsure of how to live it out concretely? This section provides clarification by showing that honoring your parents *doesn't* mean:

- pleasing
- pretending

- subjecting yourself or your children to harm
- becoming entangled in unhealthy relational patterns
- being over-responsible
- ignoring illegal, immoral, or toxic behavior

I have provided some real life examples that I hope will clarify for you how you can honor your parents without becoming mired in the mandates and dysfunction that may have accompanied what you've been taught about honor. As you read each chapter, you may find that God's Spirit is nudging you to make some changes. It may be helpful for you to sit with a journal and record your thoughts and feelings. You may be reminded of specific incidents from your childhood that were painful, confusing, or enlightening. God may ask you to revisit those places in light of his love and grace. *He sometimes takes us back in order to move us forward.*

My hope is that as we examine together what honoring doesn't mean, it will bring clarity and conviction to what it means to honor *your father and mother* in your specific life circumstances. Honoring our parents is a concept ordained by God, but it is fleshed out in the lives of real people with real issues in a real world.

Throughout this book you will read about my own journey of learning how to honor my parents. You will notice that this process is still in progress. Your process may look different than mine, but we both can take comfort in what the apostle Paul says to young Timothy: "Be diligent in these matters; give yourself wholly to them, so that everyone may see your progress" (1 Timothy 4:15 NIV).

I'm so glad that Paul didn't say, "so that everyone may see your perfection." You will find, as I did, that you will make strides toward honoring your parents one day, only to feel defeated the next as you get caught in an old, unhealthy pattern or mindset. Take heart. The process is worth it. I pray you will see God's gentle hand at work in your life and be encouraged to continue the journey. Before we begin, would you be willing to pray with me?

Dear Father, how I need Your perspective on this issue of honoring my father and mother. I feel confused and honestly dismayed at times because I want to follow Your command from an authentic humble heart. I've heard so many conflicting messages that I need Your wisdom to sort it all out. I want to lay aside all my pre-conceived notions before You and ask Your Spirit to teach me and guide me. In Jesus' name, Amen.

Chapter 1

HONORING DOESN'T MEAN PLEASING

I met Matt at a Christian university in the Midwest. He made an appointment with me after hearing me give a talk about honoring parents. As we sat down to chat, I heard in his voice an earnest desire to honor his parents, but that desire had become increasingly complicated. You see, Matt had a burden to reach people with the gospel. As a senior in high school, he had been on a short-term mission and genuinely felt God's calling to be a missionary. When he told his parents about his desire to serve God in this way, his father was furious. Although Matt came from a Christian family, his father wanted him to pursue a career in business and someday take over the family company. Matt tried on numerous occasions to talk to his father about his love of sharing his faith with people of other cultures but his father would hear nothing of it. Most recently, his father threatened to withdraw all financial support if Matt did not change his major from Cross-Cultural Evangelism to business. Matt sincerely wanted to honor his father's wishes, but admitted that he had no interest in taking over his father's business.

"Am I dishonoring my father by not taking over his business?" he asked sincerely. "If I don't change my major, am I in disobedience since my parents are paying for my education? Does honoring my parents mean that I must please them in my decisions?"

My heart went out to Matt as I listened to his dilemma. I encounter men and women of all ages and every stage of life who struggle with the same basic question: Does honoring my father and mother require that I please them?

Pressuring to Please

Most parents are not audacious enough to assert in so many words that their children need to please them in order to fulfill God's command of honoring them. But many parents do believe it and act accordingly. They exert pressure, voice their displeasure, manipulate through guilt, emotionally abandon, or act out other subtle behaviors that communicate their unspoken belief.

Don't think for a minute that I have not been there myself as a parent. There were multiple times in my daughters' growing up years that I wanted them to do what I wanted because I thought it was best. As parents, we all like to think we know our children well and that we have a corner on what would be best for them. In our overly zealous attempts to provide counsel or well-meaning advice, we exert a pressure that says, "If you don't listen and follow what I'm advising, you'll be sorry."

In the last few years, my adult daughters have reminded me of these issues. For instance, a few years ago my oldest daughter Heather she called to say she was considering returning to a job with a company she had worked for two years prior. It was a very stressful job in sales and her commission would fluctuate unpredictably. Although she loved many aspects of the job and was good at what she did, there were significant issues that caused her to quit. She phoned to say the general manager wanted to meet with her to discuss a possible job opportunity.

The minute I heard about it I was wary. I knew Heather had worked long, hard hours and profited the company while there. I also knew the demands of the job and the stress she would be under. Since she was newly married I wondered if this was the best decision.

Initially, I withheld my concern and asked what her husband Eric thought. She said they were still weighing things out, but they were considering it due to the initial salary and benefits package. We had one more conversation in which I encouraged her to carefully consider the pros and cons of the job and discuss them at length with Eric. I told her we'd be praying for them, but the most important thing was that she and Eric were on the same page.

After several weeks went by, Heather phoned again and said, "Mom, I think I'm going to take the job, even though I know you don't really want me to." I said, "Honey, it doesn't matter what I think. This is a decision between you and your husband. So, if you both feel good about it, Dad and I will support you in it."

"Mom," she choked out through tears, "everyone else in my life is really excited about it. All my friends think it will be great for me. Eric wants me to take it. I want you to be excited too."

"Heather, this is your decision and I support you in it. It's okay for you to make a decision even if I'm not fully in agreement. You're an adult and you and your husband get to make decisions together now."

"I just wish you were excited about my decision," she said, defeat in her voice.

When I hung up the phone I was a little perplexed. My other daughter Kellie, overheard the conversation. She and I started talking about it and Kellie perceptively said, "Mom, I think Heather still wants your approval."

"She doesn't need my approval; she's a married woman," I said defensively.

"Mom, even though Heather has always been one to do it her own way, I think deep down inside she longs for your approval. I think both of us are that way. Why is that, Mom?"

I stood there in silence and thought for a moment. "Kellie, that is a really good question. I think the truth is that I put a lot of pressure on both of you as little girls to do things my way. I guess on some level you still feel that pressure. I am so sorry because I know we've talked about this before."

I had several conversations with both my daughters about not having to please me, but old messages from childhood aren't easily silenced, are they? What we learn through experience is often deeply ingrained and cannot be undone with mere words. Even knowing that, I sat down to write Heather a letter.

> *My dearest Heather,*
>
> *I wanted to write to you so that you could have this in writing and re-read it often, if necessary. After our conversation today about your new job opportunity, I realized something that might help us both to grow in our relationship. I heard in your voice and your expression of sadness how much you want our approval. It became clear to me that I put a lot of pressure on you as a little girl to please me by doing what I wanted you to do. Although we've talked about this before, I realized afresh how much pressure you still feel. I am so sorry that you have carried that pressure, and on some level, you must feel that if you don't do what pleases me that it will mean a withdrawal of my love for you.*
>
> *I know I cannot undo what was done in the past, but I do want to acknowledge it and to let you know that I want you to be free from that pressure. You are no longer bound by the need to please me. You are free to be yourself. You are free to make your own decisions. You are free to be an adult who is capable of making good decisions. You are and always will be loved no matter what.*

I know these words may not "undo" what still may be in your heart, but I am hopeful that you can take some of this in. I love you Heather and want you to be free of that pressure.

You are my precious first-born daughter, whom I love beyond words. I carry you in my heart and long for you to know how much I'd love to be your friend as well as your mom.

I love you!
Mom

Nothing humbles us more than the realization that as hard as we may have tried to avoid replicating certain patterns from our own upbringing, we have inadvertently carried them with us and passed them along.

Although thirty five years had passed since my own childhood experiences of feeling pressure to please my parents, I could identify with the inner turmoil both Matt and my daughter were feeling.

A New Perspective

When I was eighteen I had a conversation with my boss over the issue of honoring my parents. It was my first "real" job, waiting tables at my best friend Lauren's family restaurant. Her father was a strong Christian man, towering over my five-foot frame at six feet, three inches. He was a stickler for making sure his employees toed the line. He approached me one afternoon and asked to meet with me after my shift was over. I racked my brain wondering where I had goofed up that day. Throughout the rest of my shift, I kept thinking, "I'm in for it now!"

To my surprise, there was a gentle tone in his voice as he said, "Janny, I have a question for you. Do you know what the Bible says your responsibility is to your parents at this stage in your life?"

"Yes," I said rather confidently. "I'm to honor and obey them."

"That's true, the Bible does say that children are to obey their parents and that is how they show them honor. Now that you're an adult, what do you think it means?"

"I guess the same thing. Since I'm still living at home I have to obey them and not do anything that displeases them."

He pulled out his Bible and turned to Ephesians 6: 1–2, and asked me to read it aloud. He proceeded to show me from Scripture that as a child I had a clear responsibility to obey my parents.

"But," he said, "now that you are an adult, your responsibility shifts to that of honoring them."

I was confused. In my family, honoring meant obeying what my parents said, but it also meant pleasing them and not making decisions that were contrary to what they thought was best.

As I expressed my confusion, tears started rolling down my face. There had been several instances lately in which I felt as though I had disappointed my parents. Most of those situations centered around me wanting to attend a mid-week Bible study at my boyfriend's home, or spending time at Lauren's house, or not spending enough time at home with the family. My parents would not forbid me to go, but made it clear that they would prefer I make the choice to stay home. This led to tremendous inner conflict. I didn't think some of what I wanted was unreasonable, but since I wanted to be an obedient daughter I felt compelled to comply. I now know that Lauren must have shared with her dad the emotional turmoil I was in.

"Janny," he said tenderly but firmly, "now that you are an adult, you are directly responsible to God. Since you are living in your parent's home you must be considerate and respectful, contribute to household responsibilities, and honor your parents. But you are not under obligation always to please your parents. The Bible does not require that of you, nor does God expect that from you."

I could hardly believe my ears. I felt an immediate burden lift off my shoulders. Could this really be true? Was I free from the weight of always trying to make sure my parents were "pleased" by my behavior and decisions? Could I actually be accountable to God and his Word directly? I sensed, even then, the freedom and the tremendous responsibility that this new paradigm presented. God desired me to continue to honor my parents but now I had the responsibility to find out what was pleasing to *God*. I did not take this lightly. It caused me to want to study and learn what Scripture had to say about how I should conduct my life.

Trying to sort out this new idea was challenging. If I wasn't responsible to *please* my parents, what would it look like to honor them? If I made a decision that displeased my parents, was I to hide it from them in order to "keep the peace"? If I was open about my decision, how was I going to deal with their displeasure? What if I made a decision that turned out to be wrong? How could I make my parents understand that I wasn't trying to hurt them or disrespect them, but was simply trying to learn to make decisions on my own while seeking God for direction?

Learn by Doing

I am an experiential learner. Throughout my life, God seems to allow or sometimes orchestrate circumstances so that He might teach me a principle or instruct me. I've found that most of my walk with God has unfolded in this way.

Soon after turning eighteen, I met a young man named Randy who was a regular patron at the restaurant in which I worked. Randy was twenty five years old, respectful, kind, and had a good job.

After several months, Randy asked me out on a date. I knew this would be problematic. I knew my parents would never go for me dating someone "that old." My parents' rule required that I only date guys no more than two years my senior. Strike number one against Randy.

Then, there was the issue of his hair. As was common in the 70s, Randy's hair hit the top of his collared shirt, which would definitely be out of the question. Strike number two against "hippie man."

The final disqualifier was Randy's living situation. He had his own apartment that he shared with a friend. Strike number three against the "bachelor pad." I was in turmoil. I wanted to date Randy. I knew in my heart he was a good man with integrity and that I would be treated with respect. I also knew what my dad would say. What should I do?

I approached my parents and asked if Randy could come over to meet them. My dad asked the particulars: Who is he? Where did you meet him? How old is he? And that was the end of that discussion.

Shortly thereafter, my grandparents were visiting from Indiana. Although we didn't see them often, I was very fond of grandfather Ray. What I remember most about him was his booming voice, his laughter, and his love of God's Word.

I remember talking with him one afternoon about my desire to date Randy. I told him that my dad refused my request in no uncertain terms. My grandpa sat thoughtfully for a few minutes and then offered a suggestion: "I think you should go to your dad again. This time, tell him respectfully that you don't agree with his decision. Tell him that you believe Randy is a good young man whom he would approve of if he knew him. Tell him that you are not going to sneak around behind his back and see Randy, even though you could. Then tell him that you will abide by his decision because you want to honor God, even though you don't agree with him."

I did go to my dad as my grandpa suggested and in less than a month, out of the blue one day my dad said, "If you want to date that old man, I guess it's okay with me." I almost fell over on the dining room floor. I never knew if my grandpa talked with my dad or if grandpa just prayed. I ended up dating Randy for over a year and my parents really liked him.

But I never forgot the lesson that God seemed to be teaching me: as an adult, it is perfectly acceptable to disagree with your parents and choose your own path as long as you do so respectfully. I don't know what I would have done had my dad not changed his mind. But I do know I was one step further in the process of learning to openly address differences of opinion with my parents and risk disapproval. I was learning that change had to start with me.

Change Begins with Me

This experience was the turning point in beginning to understand the difference between honoring my parents through obedience as a child and what it would look like as I moved into maturity as an adult. It was especially difficult for me in the early years of adulthood because my parents' model of honor had **not** changed. Their view morphed from requiring absolute obedience from me as a child to expecting compliance with their opinions and wishes as I became a young adult. It became clear that if this model was to change it had to begin with me.

I was learning how to shift my accountability from my parents directly to God. This was not as easy as it might sound because up to that point in my life my parents had taught me to believe that following their wishes was the *same* as following God's. In some families this is what is expected. Back then, I didn't have at my fingertips the resources we have today; books about dysfunctional family systems, healthy versus unhealthy parenting styles, or what it means to function as an adult. What I did have was the Spirit of God within me gently guiding me and instructing me through His Word and examples from other people like my boss and my grandpa.

I was on the verge of making a break-through.

Honoring Doesn't Mean Pleasing

After I put myself through college, I obtained a job working for the county as a counselor at a juvenile facility. I was living independently from my parents and needed a new car desperately. I was approved for a car loan through my local credit union so I began the process of looking for a new vehicle. This was in the 70s and I was enamored with a new model of car that had just been released: a Honda Civic. It was the first generation of Hondas and although quite small it promised reliability, great gas mileage, an AM radio and it cost under $3,000.

I was excited about the car and went to talk with my parents about the purchase. My dad was very vocal about his displeasure. "We buy American in this family," he said emphatically, and any attempt to discuss my reasoning or thought process was immediately quelled. I left their home deflated. I had been so excited about the purchase and so proud of myself that I was in a position to purchase a brand new car on my own, but their disapproval was disheartening.

I decided not to abandon the idea but to pray and seek God's wisdom. Since I was financially independent, living on my own, and driving over sixty miles per day to work, it seemed like a prudent purchase. I still was in some internal turmoil knowing that my parents would not approve. I couldn't quite escape the feeling that if I bought the car without their approval, it would be destined to be a "bad" car that would prove to me I "should have listened to my parents." But the more I prayed about it, the more it seemed like God was giving me the freedom to make my own choice. It was not a choice of rebellion against my parents, but a choice for me and my ability to make reasonable decisions for myself. I bought the car and soon after there was an oil crisis that hit, causing the cost of gasoline to spike. Since the Hondas were among the few newer cars on the market that took regular gas, it proved to be an added blessing. Although my parents were initially displeased by the purchase, I was able to settle in my own heart that I could make decisions on my own and risk their disapproval.

Relating Adult to Adult

Sometimes it is difficult for parents and adult children to make the transition from a parent/child relationship to an adult-to-adult relationship. One author writes, "If you have a child's perspective or feel powerless when dealing with your parents, you may find yourself trying to avoid making a scene, fearing confrontations and avoiding any emotional issues, or thinking that it is not worth the trouble because your parents will sooner or later be gone. Even though you may accuse your parents of 'forcing you' to submit to their wishes, the actuality is that you *choose* to give up your power by the way you view the relationship."[1]

To honor one's parents means to treat them with respect; it does not mean gratifying their every wish or being agreeable for the sake of avoiding their displeasure. I have known people well into adulthood who are still stuck in this mind-set. I have great compassion for them because I know how difficult it is to shift your thinking and change your behavior. But the cost of not doing so is often reflected in other circles of one's life. I came across this quote that talks about this very thing:

> If you take your parents' expectations and conditions too seriously, your daily life will be filled with attempts to resist or give in to their values. Such either/or thinking implies 'Either do what they say or you will lose their love and respect.' It is not surprising to find that people in their forties, fifties, and sixties continue to work themselves to death, to resent their bosses, and to feel unfulfilled because they are subconsciously still trying to please their parents.[2]

So what does it look like to relate to your parents adult to adult? I think one of the most important aspects of being able to relate to your parents as an adult is—*to be one*. In other words, be an adult yourself. Take responsibility for your decisions, values, time, finances, feelings, opinions, dreams, limitations, attitudes, and behavior. Whether your parents recognize your adulthood and treat you as such, you act like an adult in your life and in relationship to them. This means that you give them what you want from them as well; things like respect, consideration, rights to their own decisions and opinions, freedom rather than manipulation, space instead of dependence, honesty, compassion, and patience.

We will explore more about what it looks like to have an adult to adult relationship in Chapter 4, but before we leave this topic, let's briefly explore what this adult to adult relationship looks like as our parents age and why it is so important that these issues of relating as adults is a well-established pattern.

Parenting Our Parents

Many of us realize that as our parents age the roles reverse. We are often in the position of having to "parent" our aging parents. We must be willing to consider their opinions but also look out for their welfare. In some families this is extremely difficult. We may find ourselves in a situation with our parent that resembles a tantrum by a two year-old who screams, "By myself!" Or it may resemble the adolescent who rages, "I am old enough to make my own decisions! I don't need your help!" We have to find the strength, compassion, and wisdom to navigate these situations just as we would if our parent was really that age. It means that we resist the power struggle by validating their desire to be independent while presenting the reality of their limitations and we invite dialogue in which different options can be considered collectively.

Understanding this is especially critical as one's parents age because children are often in the position of having to offer care or financial assistance in their parents' latter years.

After my husband Don's father passed away, his mother lived by herself in their home. Because she was unable to drive due to a medical condition, it became necessary for family members to assist by driving her to doctor's appointments. Her daughter lived with her for several years, and she provided some of her care, as did I.

But with the onset of significant health issues and several emergency room visits in the middle of the night, we as a family knew it was time for my mother-in-law to live with one of her children. We offered our home, as did my sister-in-law, but my mother-in-law initially rejected both offers. Another emergency room visit soon followed.

Finally, we said to her that we were concerned for her safety due to her inability to care properly for herself. Her refusal to live elsewhere was becoming a hardship for those of us who lived far enough away that we couldn't get to her quickly or easily. Thankfully, she was cooperative and she agreed to live with my sister-in-law. She was initially very depressed when she had to leave her home, but we knew this was the best decision in the long run both for her and for family members who were providing for her care.

Genuine honor means that we listen to their views respectfully, consider their opinions, and give weight to their perspective even when it differs from our own. But if we placate our parents with our behavior while holding them in contempt in our hearts, this is anything but honorable. That kind of duplicitous life is what Jesus indicted the Pharisees for continually in the New Testament: "These people honor me with their lips, but their hearts are far from me" (Matthew 15:8 NIV).

Learning how to honor your parents without feeling compelled to please them in every decision can be difficult. It is a process that may include having an honest discussion with your parents. It may look something like this: "Mom and Dad, I want you to know how much I appreciate your experience in life and the wisdom you've gained. I think I'm well-prepared to make good decisions, even though I know I'll make mistakes. From time to time, I may ask for your advice and feedback concerning a decision I have to make. I want you to know that your opinion means something to me and I will consider it carefully. Just know that since I'm now an adult these decisions rest on my shoulders. I may disappoint you by doing something different than what you recommend, but I'm confident that this is part of the process of being an adult. Thanks for your support and respect."

This kind of honest conversation may not produce a welcome response, but it is a healthy step in the process of learning how to honor your parents without necessarily pleasing them.

Chapter 2

HONORING DOESN'T MEAN PRETENDING

Several years ago, a popular Christian radio host by the name of Rich Buhler had a talk show titled "Talk from the Heart." For several hours each afternoon, Rich would take callers who wanted his down-to earth, biblically-based advice about their specific situation.

A caller phoned in one day and asked Rich how in the world he was supposed to "honor his father and mother" when his father was a raging alcoholic and his mother had spent her life making excuses for him at the expense of this caller and his five siblings. He went on to say he could find nothing honorable about the way they lived, and in fact, he could only remember one time that his father said something half-way nice to him.

"Does God really expect me to honor him? How can I honor them when they've acted so dishonorably toward me and my brothers and sisters?" he asked sincerely.

Rich's reply was simple but profound and I've never forgotten it. He said, "The way we honor our parents as adults is similar to what we do with past presidents of the United States. We can honor the position this person has held without agreeing or supporting everything their administration stood for."[1]

So it is with our parents. It is possible to honor our parents and the position they were given by God without condoning, excusing or pretending that bad things did not happen.[1] Charles Sell in his book, *Unfinished Business,* writes, "Truth is the issue, not love or loyalty. Love covers a multitude of sins, but it should not distort them."[2]

Image Control

Sometimes as Christians we think we are dishonoring our parents if we talk about anything that might put them in a bad light. We might have been given messages in our family not to "air the family's dirty laundry in public." Or as one woman describing what honor meant in her home said, "[It meant] don't answer back; don't raise your voice to them; don't drag family 'stuff' into public view; protect their reputation. Especially since my dad was pastor of a church!"

I don't know why we think we have to present a flawless image to the world. In fact, we certainly don't learn that when we read Scripture. I think one of the things I most love about Scripture is that it is full of truth—not just doctrinal truth but truths to live by on a day-to-day basis. God, in his Word, tells the truth about people. As we read through Scripture we find people who are just like us—people who've made mistakes, sinned against God and others, failed as parents to guide their children wisely, and people whose lives looked hopeless but for the grace of God.

I love that God didn't give us examples of just the "successes." He gives us the whole picture of some of his most esteemed followers:

- Abraham, the liar whose lying tendencies passed on to his son, was called "the friend of God"
- Moses, whose anger kept him out of the Promised Land, was a man whom God talked to "face to face"

- Rahab, the harlot of Jericho who saved the spies who were checking out Canaan, would be in the genealogy of Jesus, the Messiah
- David, the murderer, adulterer, and passive father was called "a man after God's own heart"
- Samuel, the neglectful father who didn't restrain his sons, was also one of the greatest prophets and leaders Israel had ever known
- The Woman at the Well in John 4, a woman who was living in sin and had a history of five previous marriages, became a woman whose life and community were transformed because she declared to everyone she knew that Jesus was surely the long-awaited Messiah

Truth that Sets us Free

Yes, God is able to transform and restore any life no matter what we've experienced, but it all starts with dealing with the truth and not pretending. "Pretending is a lot of work," wrote Rich Buhler in his hallmark book.[3] God isn't interested in the ideals; He works with realities and restores people by His grace that are willing to believe Him, hold onto His Word and deal with the truth. In John 8:31–32 we read, "If you hold to my teaching, you are really my disciples. Then you will know the truth, and the truth will set you free" (NIV).

Many years ago in my counseling practice a woman came to me seeking help regarding her relationship with her father. For years her father had doted on her, an only child. Her father seemed to almost be obsessed with making sure she thought of him as a wonderful, caring dad and grandfather. He went overboard picking up little presents for her and her kids, making sure he was at sporting events, and just being the father and grandfather that all her friends envied.

In the course of treatment, she began remembering incidents that seemed totally incongruent with the father she knew. There was sexual abuse, not only with her, but also with other members of her extended family. She almost couldn't believe these memories could be true. How could her father have done these things? How could he live with himself and pretend to be something he was not?

I'll never forget her saying to me, "This can't be true. I must be making this up or I must be crazy." Her father began molesting her at around age four, but then he spent a lifetime pretending to be the "perfect father" in case she remembered.

What is so amazing about this woman's story is the healing that came about because she was willing to deal with the truth. Facing the truth of what happened allowed her to see issues that needed to be dealt with and boundaries that needed to be in place for the protection of her own children. It also helped her to understand her parents and the dynamics of their relationship that had always been confusing and hurtful to her as a child. In spite of her father's refusal to admit what he'd done to her and others, she was able to forgive him and work toward a healthier relationship with both her parents.

I've seen over the years how detrimental pretending can be. It can take a toll on a person's physical health as well as their emotional and mental well being. God doesn't ask us to pretend for the sake of honoring. He asks us to honor our parents even in light of what is true. That kind of honor doesn't minimize, excuse, or annihilate truth; it simply acknowledges it and chooses to respect those who are in the God-given position of being our parents.

I remember well the emotional turmoil that each holiday would evoke when I was a young wife and mother. Even though my relationship with my parents had been peaceable for several years, I was an emotional wreck in anticipation of being with them. This seemed to make no sense—our time together would usually consist of having a pleasant time of conversation around the dinner table, and there were no conflicts or harsh words. In the course of a year, we would see my parents five or six times, and as each time approached, I found myself being short with my daughter, irritable with my husband, and suffering some depression and anxiety.

I remember praying and asking God to help me with these feelings. One day, I realized what was causing such angst. It was all about *pretending*. The emotional energy that it took to be with my parents without ever having spoken about the abuse in our home was absolutely taking its toll on me. Pretending took emotional energy. It was like trying to hold dozens of helium-filled balloons under water all at once. I just couldn't do it. I realized I was hurting my husband, my daughter, and myself by trying to put on a smiling face for the sake of not upsetting the family. After seeking counsel from several wise people, I was encouraged to take a "time-out" from seeing my parents for the purpose of healing.

That period of time proved to be so beneficial to me, but also to my parents. God was working behind the scenes in my parents as well, preparing the soil of their hearts to hear the truth from me about what took place in our family. I eventually sat down with both my parents and talked about the sexual abuse perpetrated by my stepfather and the impact it had on my life. I've detailed that conversation in my book *Door of Hope*. There was truth spoken for the first time and from then on there was to be no pretending. I could not control their denial as it concerned their other relationships, but it was clear that when we were together we would not pretend those things had not happened. It also didn't mean that each time we were with them that we talked about the abuse; it just meant that we were not going to pretend we had a different family than we did. The process of dealing with what was true in our family led to a restoration with my parents that lasted throughout their lives. I know this would have not been possible were it not for the abundance of God's grace and mercy toward us all.

Honoring in Truth

"I'm done pretending! I can't do it anymore. No matter how my dad wants to distort the truth, it is what it is!" said Marcus in a determined tone. Marcus wanted to talk to me about his situation. He was married, in his mid-30s, with two children. His parents lived two hours away and were hurt that he did not visit them more often. Over the years he offered different legitimate excuses: stress at his job, home projects that were long overdue, the kids' sporting events, whatever he could to lengthen his time between visits.

"What makes your visits so uncomfortable?" I asked.

"It's my mom. It is an endless barrage of guilt manipulation and criticism. She pours it on from the moment I step in the door until we're on the driveway backing our car out. *'I just don't understand why you can't call or visit more often. All your other brothers and sisters make time for us. We've done so much for you and this is what we get? You are not the son that I always thought you would be. You're such a disappointment . . .*" he said in a whiny, mimicking tone.

I was surprised. "I thought you were upset with your dad. I can hear you have a lot of hurt from your mom."

"Well, I guess I'm upset with both of them, but more so with my dad because of all the excuses he makes for her. I know my dad has lived with 'her ways' for forty two years, but I've had it. My dad thinks I just need to overlook the constant criticism and her berating me in front of everyone. My dad emailed me and said I am overreacting and that all mom's criticisms are from a heart that is pure. He said I'm dishonoring her by not accepting her 'advice' because she just wants the best for my family and me. Dad is asking me to pretend that her words don't hurt me, but they do!"

I could tell Marcus was pouring out years of frustration. It wasn't just about their most recent encounter. I wasn't only hearing the thirty-eight-year-old man whose mother wished he'd visit more. I was hearing the eight-year-old little boy inside him whose heart had been wounded by a lifetime of mom's critical judgments and harsh pronouncements. I heard the frustration of a little boy who wished his father would stop pretending and stand up for him.

No matter whether we find ourselves pretending for the sake of the family's image or we feel pressure to pretend from family members who don't want to face the truth, we can choose not to pretend.

We cannot change anyone else. We cannot force people to see things our way or see a situation in reality. We *can* stop pretending ourselves and with God's help deal with what is true. When we are willing to do this and begin the process of working through the grief about what happened, healing can begin. As we grieve through the pain of what was, and the losses that resulted, we can move through to forgiveness and learn to accept what is. This is the way to genuine honor.

The word *honor* implies integrity. We often apply that only to the person to whom we give honor, but I think it also applies to the one who gives it. If we are truly going to honor our parents, it must have authenticity and the kind of integrity that says, "I honor you for the position you hold, recognizing you were placed in my life by God, used by Him in spite of your failures, sins, and weaknesses, to help develop in me the character and life that will bring praise and glory to God. For that I give you honor, and in so doing, I seek humbly to honor God."

Honoring doesn't mean we have to pretend that bad things did not happen. Pretending may preserve the status quo, but it never serves the pretender. As we seek to honor our parents, there must be a balance of both truth and grace. Randy Alcorn says it best:

> Grace and truth are both necessary. Neither is sufficient.... We who are truth-oriented need to go out of our way to affirm grace. We who are grace-oriented need to go out of our way to affirm truth. "Hate the sin, but love the sinner." No one did either like Jesus. Truth hates sin. Grace loves sinners. Those full of grace and truth do both.[4]

Chapter 3

HONORING DOESN'T MEAN SUBJECTING YOURSELF OR YOUR CHILDREN TO HARM

My husband Don's father was an alcoholic. But it wasn't until Don was twenty-seven that he realized it. We were dating at the time and he was sharing with me over the phone about the most recent episode with his father's drinking that caused him to lose his job. As a probation officer, I had taken several training sessions on substance abuse. I remember saying to Don, "Your father is an alcoholic." A long silence followed.

"Don, until your dad is willing to go to AA and admit he has a problem, these kinds of things are going to continue to happen. You can't fix this on your own." I could tell Don was in shock. None of his six brothers and sisters had ever talked about his dad's drinking. They all experienced the fallout, but no one, including their mother, had ever called it what it was.

Don and I were married in 1979 in Riverside, California. In the middle of our reception at the historic Mission Inn, we could not find Don's father for a photograph. Tim, one of Don's groomsmen and a family friend, found Don's dad getting drunk in a bar downstairs. That was only a shadow of things to come. He continued to drink and refused to get help. Before his death in 1991, despite numerous detoxes, he never admitted to being an alcoholic and refused to attend AA because he was "not like those people."

Early in our marriage, when our daughters were three and five, Don and I drove over to Don's parents' home one afternoon for a visit. When we walked in, I saw Don's father sitting in his lounge chair in a stupor. His clothes were dirty, he was unshaven, and it looked like he hadn't bathed in days. A bottle of booze sat on the floor beside him, and his trousers were unzipped. I diverted my daughters' attention to their grandmother and let Don know discreetly that we needed to leave—immediately.

As we walked to our car, I said, "Don, I will not subject our girls to that. If your mom wants to live that way, that is her choice, but I refuse to expose our girls to your father in that state. If your mom wants to visit the girls, we will come and pick her up and take her to our house, but I'm not doing this again."

This kind of response was uncommon in Don's family. Everyone in Don's family, as in most alcoholic families, had adapted to their father's alcoholism by simply ignoring it. Don remembers as a young teen hearing his mother and father arguing late into the night over his dad's drinking. He would lie in bed fearing his father might get violent with his mother. The next morning all the kids would get up, having heard the fight the previous night. But no one would speak a word about it and life went on. As children, we often don't have a lot of options when it comes to our family situation. We grow accustomed to our experience and find ways to adapt. But once we become adults, we have opportunities to respond to our family situation in healthier, more constructive ways.

Sometimes it is necessary for the sake of protection to employ safeguards or boundaries that keep you or your children from harm. This doesn't mean you are dishonoring your parents. They may be dishonoring themselves by their behavior, but it doesn't mean you have to participate and it doesn't mean you have to sever relationship completely.

Because of the sexual abuse in my background and the alcoholism of Don's father, it was clear that boundaries needed to be in set in our family's relationship with both sets of parents. Don and I loved them dearly, but we wanted to break the generational cycle of alcoholism and abuse. And this meant instituting some safeguards. When I confronted my stepfather about the sexual abuse in our home, I gently made it clear that my daughters would never stay in their home. Although I genuinely forgave my stepfather, I knew I had to take steps to insure my daughters' protection. I did not want my girls to come to me in twenty years and say, "Mom, why did you let us stay at grandma and grandpa's house, knowing what you knew?" Even though my stepfather assured me that he would "never molest" my daughters, I said, "Dad, that is not good enough. You know you would have said those same words twenty five years ago." I knew in my heart that this was not a lack of forgiveness on my part; it was a step of wisdom. We maintained that boundary throughout our daughters' childhoods and have no regrets. We were able to have a loving relationship with my parents for over twenty years with those limits in place, due to God's grace and wisdom.

In this chapter, we're going to see that honoring doesn't mean that we subject ourselves or our children to harm. We will explore what circumstances might require safeguards, what purpose safeguards serve, and how it is possible to set limits and maintain honor from a Biblical perspective.

What Circumstances Require Safeguards?

You may be wondering what circumstances warrant safeguards or what constitutes "harm." Webster's defines *harm* as "physical or mental damage: injury" and *harmful* as "of a kind likely to be damaging: injurious."[1] In certain situations this is very clear cut: When the potential of physical harm exists, when you or your children are exposed to verbal or emotional abuse, or when an environment is likely to produce high levels of duress or anxiety.

Dr. Susan Forward, in her book, *Toxic Parents,* writes that many people have difficult relationships with their parents. "[But] that alone doesn't mean that your parents are emotionally destructive."[2] In trying to find a word that best described parents whose behavior might warrant safeguards, Dr. Forward writes, "What better word than *toxic* to describe parents who inflict ongoing trauma, abuse, and denigration on their children and in most cases continue to do so even after their children are grown?"[3] Dr. Forward acknowledges that all of us as parents are deficient at times because we're human, "[b]ut there are many parents whose negative patterns of behavior are consistent and dominant in a child's life. These are the parents who do the harm."[4]

Other family situations are more subjective and ambiguous when it comes to requiring safeguards. This is partially because we can become so accustomed to life and relationships within our family that we often aren't able to see things for what they really are. As children, the environment in which we grow up becomes our "normal." Rarely do we evaluate our family or relationships as children; we simply absorb them. That is why it is helpful as adults to get an outside perspective to help us evaluate what is or is not harmful and what steps can or should be taken to insure our well being and the safety of our children.

Justin and Lori came to see me for just this reason. They had been married three years and had two small children. As we sat down together, Justin shared about his family history. His parents divorced when he was six and his sister was four. His mother remarried two years later and his stepfather is the only father figure he's really ever known. His mother was emotionally unstable and often tried to manipulate Justin and his sister through guilt.

This pattern continued into his adulthood. If they didn't visit enough, she would tearfully accuse him of keeping the grandchildren from her. If the tears didn't work, she would get angry and tell him what a "selfish, ungrateful boy" he'd always been. If that didn't seem to do the trick, she would call several relatives telling them how badly she was being treated and then Justin would get a barrage of phone calls and letters indicting him for not honoring his parents. Justin usually ended up apologizing to his mom and all would be forgiven—until the next time he didn't meet her expectations and it would start all over again.

Of greatest concern to Justin and Lori was a recent development. A cousin had recently informed them that Justin's stepfather molested her when she was a child. Her counselor had advised her to inform family members with children about the abuse. One day, while visiting his parents' home, Justin opened a drawer trying to locate the television remote only to find some pornographic material. He and Lori were very troubled by these findings and ended up discussing the issues with his mom and stepfather. The discussion ended poorly.

Feeling at a loss, Justin and Lori told Justin's parents that they did not feel comfortable leaving the children in their care. Justin's mom went ballistic, accusing the cousin of discrediting her husband, berating Justin for believing such things in light of "how good your dad has always been to you," and making it clear that if they weren't allowed to see their grandchildren they might pursue legal action, suing for grandparents' rights.

In the following months, Justin and Lori made several attempts to reconcile by offering alternatives such as meeting his parents at a park where they could spend time with the children with Justin and Lori present. Their hope was that in time there could be more discussion and opportunities to build trust. Even though his parents initially agreed to these arrangements, they failed to show up on several occasions and then told extended family members that Justin was part of a religious cult that was prohibiting their contact with their grandchildren. To Justin and Lori's credit, they attempted to maintain connection with Justin's parents, but as time went on, it became clear that his parents weren't willing to go through the necessary process of reconciliation.

Unfortunately, there are situations that demand we take steps of protection for ourselves as well as our children—even if these safeguards lead to tensions like those experienced by Justin and Lori.

What Purposes Do Safeguards Serve?

Safeguards serve several purposes. As we just saw in Justin and Lori's situation, safeguards serve the purpose of *protection*. This doesn't mean that we need to become hyper-vigilant. We don't need to obsess over every potential harm that our children might encounter from family members. It does mean that we exercise wisdom and discernment as we carefully and prayerfully seek God's balance in honoring our parents while at the same time protecting our children's well being.

Sometimes safeguards should be implemented for what might be called *seasons of healing*. There is something to be said for giving ourselves time and space to pursue growth, maturity, and emotional healing. For some, this can be done without interrupting family connections, but for others it isn't so easy.

As I sat with Erica over lunch, I could see the anguish on her face. She had recently graduated from college and had called me because she was not sure what to do. Her parents had divorced when she was fifteen and both had remarried. She enjoyed a good relationship with her mother and stepfather, but her relationship with her father was strained. His alcoholism and emotional outbursts often triggered some unresolved hurts from her childhood that left her feeling vulnerable and confused. Her father insisted that he and his wife have "equal time" to that of her mother and stepfather following her graduation ceremony. He reminded her of his financial contribution to her education and told her how she had hurt him and his wife on more than one occasion due to her lack of appreciation for all they had done.

"Erica," I asked, "if you could do what *you* really wanted to do in relation to your father, what would you do?"

"I'd want him to admit that he has a problem with alcohol and be honest about how his anger hurt me growing up."

"Erica, you just told me what you wanted *from* your father. I'm asking what *you* really want to do concerning the relationship with your father."

She missed the question again and reiterated how she wished her father would be willing to take ownership of how destructive his temper had been in their family.

"Erica" I said gently, "I don't want you to think about how anyone else will feel or react. I just want you to think about what you want. If you could do absolutely anything you wanted to do as it concerned your father, what would you do?"

With tears in her eyes, she simply said, "I'd stop seeing or talking to him for a while."

I nodded my head and acknowledged her honest answer. As we continued our conversation over the next hour, Erica shared how difficult it was to have a relationship with her father. It seemed that whenever she didn't do things his way, he became angry or tried to induce guilt. She confessed that she went through times where she would withdraw without a word after some difference of opinion just to avoid the conflict. This estrangement was invariably followed by a letter of chastisement from her father who made it clear that he was very hurt and confused and that she was not "honoring" him as her father.

It was clear from our time together that Erica needed to enter a *season of healing*. She needed to come to grips with the effects of her father's alcoholism, grieve through the losses of the divorce, and gain support from others who could help her develop in her growth as an adult. We talked about how it wasn't going to help if she simply stopped seeing her dad for a while unless she used that time in a proactive way. She would need to make this season of healing productive not just by "removing" someone who was hurtful, but by "adding" others who understood and could support her growth.

In their book *Boundaries*, Drs. Cloud and Townsend write, "Emotional distance is a temporary boundary to give your heart the space it needs to be safe; it is never a permanent way of living. People who have been in abusive relationships need to find a safe place to begin to 'thaw out' emotionally. You should not continue to set yourself up for hurt and disappointment."[5]

It's important to say here that we must take responsibility for our own responses and our own healing. Too many times we either stay in destructive relationships with parents hoping that they will "see the light" and change, or we step back from relationship as a means to get our point across, thinking that separation will be the motivation that will make *them* want to change. Both of these stances will not produce change because they are "other-oriented." We are responsible for our own heart attitudes, our behavior, and our emotional growth and healing.

If we are seeking God and the wise counsel of others and it seems fitting to take a "time-out" from a parent for the purpose of healing, we must actively pursue that healing through joining a support group, seeking professional counseling, obtaining pastoral guidance or spiritual direction, or spending time with others who can assist us in the grieving and forgiveness process. Failing to enter proactively into a season of healing will only cause the hurtful issues to lie dormant, only to reemerge unexpectedly.

Setting Safeguards Doesn't Mean Avoiding

Sometimes we fail to set appropriate safeguards out of a misguided notion that to do so would constitute a failure to embrace family duties. But setting safeguards, when done properly, is not the same thing as avoiding.

Sara was beside herself. She had recently invited her father, a widower, to live in her home. She talked with her husband and teenage children about the move and tried to prepare them for the adjustment. Her husband was initially supportive, but within a few short weeks, everyone was in turmoil.

Sara had been abused by her father growing up but never talked to him about it. Her father had a drinking problem during those years, but had since stopped drinking. Sara shared with her husband and siblings about the abuse, but not her children. Just prior to her father moving in, her teenagers found out about the abuse from a relative. They were angry with Sara for never talking with them about this—and they couldn't believe that she was considering having their grandfather move in. Although they vocalized their concerns, Sara felt it was her "duty" to care for her father.

Sara admitted that since her father had moved in, no one was happy. Her father was sullen and often holed up in his room, her teenagers were frustrated that they had to share the bathroom with grandpa, and her husband felt neglected. Sara confessed that she was having panic attacks and suffered from migraines and insomnia. She felt caught in the middle and was upset with her family for not understanding and making an effort to make the living situation workable.

I have talked to so many people who feel this same dilemma. They want to honor their parents but find themselves assailed by issues that they have not dealt with adequately. Sara's sincere desire to care for her father was honorable. However, carrying out that desire was significantly challenged because she tried to release some things she'd never really embraced. Sara needed to learn that it is possible to honor her duties toward her father even while maintaining safeguards in their relationship.

Honoring with Safeguards

Although the Bible does not explicitly address what we do with an alcoholic or abusive parent, there are principles that we can glean from Scripture about honoring our parents while at the same time instituting appropriate safeguards.

In the Old Testament there is a story of the relationship between King Saul and David. King Saul was Israel's first king. After Saul's blatant disobedience, Samuel the prophet tells Saul that God is removing him as king. God directs Samuel to the shepherd boy David whom he anoints as the next king of Israel. David's fame and popularity increase when he defeats the Philistine giant Goliath, causing King Saul to become jealous.

King Saul realizes God's favor rests upon David and not on him, and he devises military plans to jeopardize David's life. When all of his schemes fail, King Saul initiates a relentless pursuit of David over a ten-year period that is recorded in 1 Samuel, chapters 18 through 26. It should be noted that David is King Saul's son-in-law, which makes this situation a "family affair."

There are two incidents recorded in which David is given an opportunity to kill King Saul: one in 1 Samuel 24, the other in chapter 26. Both times David's men recommend that David take advantage of this fortuitous opportunity. In the first instance, David responds by saying, "The LORD forbid that I should do such a thing to my master, the LORD's anointed, or lay my hand on him; for he is the anointed of the LORD " (1 Samuel 24:6 NIV). Later, David addresses Saul directly with these words:

> "This day have you seen with your own eyes how the LORD delivered you into my hands in the cave. Some urged me to kill you, but I spared you; I said, 'I will not lay my hand on my LORD, because he is the LORD's anointed.' See, my father, look at this

piece of your robe in my hand! I cut off the corner of your robe but did not kill you. See that there is nothing in my hand to indicate that I am guilty of wrongdoing or rebellion. I have not wronged you, but you are hunting me down to take my life. May the Lord judge between you and me. And may the Lord avenge the wrongs you have done to me, but my hand will not touch you. As the old saying goes, 'From evildoers come evil deeds,' so my hand will not touch you" (1 Samuel 24:10–13 niv)

The story concludes with King Saul's tragic death and David's lament over the loss of the king.

What can we learn from this? Is there anything in this story that we can apply to the relationship with our parents? First, it is important to note that David sought to be reconciled with King Saul. On more than one occasion, David pleaded with the king to hear the genuineness of his heart and loyalty. When these appeals were rebuffed, David did not continue to subject himself to harm or danger. He sought refuge and took appropriate steps to insure his safety. Next, we see that David did not take matters into his own hands when the opportunity for a vengeful response presented itself. Instead, he modeled respect for King Saul's God-given position. Even though David would have been totally justified in taking Saul's life according to his military companions, he would not act in a retaliatory way. He submitted himself and King Saul to the only One who fairly judges men's hearts.

Most of us will never be in a situation where we are literally being "hunted down." But David's experience can teach us a few things. Like David, we may be in a situation with a parent that warrants safety measures. We may have appealed to our parent with little result and we may need to take steps to insure our physical or emotional safety or that of our children. We may even need to remove ourselves from contact for a period of time.

Sometimes it's helpful to set safeguards. Some people view boundaries as limits we "put on others," but in reality, healthy boundaries are limits we set for ourselves. We can limit our exposure to people who have a history of treating us poorly. We can't change them or require them to treat us differently, but we can separate ourselves from those who act in hurtful ways toward us.

It should be noted that David and King Saul never fully reconciled their relationship. There are some relationships with parents in which reconciliation is not feasible. "We are not required as an act of obedience to reconcile. We are required as an act of obedience to forgive."[6] Forgiveness is God's prescription to insure our freedom, but restoration in some relationships is not always possible. God does not hold us accountable for restoration; He says, "If it is possible, as far as it depends on you, live at peace with everyone" (Romans 12:18 NIV).

Like David, we can choose to honor the God-given position our parents have as we talked about in the last chapter. Rather than seeking revenge, we submit and entrust ourselves and our parents to God whose sovereignty perfectly balances justice and mercy.

Don and I both came from families where it was necessary to set safeguards. It didn't mean that relationship had to end. It was through setting limits and boundaries that we were free to love and maintain relationship with our parents throughout their lives. I'm so grateful for God's gracious redemption—He's a God who sets limits, but He is limitless in his love to those who put their trust in Him.

Chapter 4

HONORING DOESN'T MEAN BECOMING ENTANGLED IN UNHEALTHY RELATIONAL PATTERNS

"Hi Mom," I said cheerfully. "I'm calling to invite you and Dad to our Christmas brunch. We've invited family and friends so there is a great mix of people and it'll be a nice relaxing time. We'd love for you to come."

"Well, I'll look at the calendar to see what we have that day," my Mom said.

"Mom, I want you to know that I've invited Bill and his woman friend too."

There was a long pause. I had dared to speak my natural father's name to my mother, not to mention invite him to the same event.

"Well," my mother said coolly, "if *he* comes to your brunch, your dad and I will not be coming."

"Mom, I would really like you to come, but if you decide not to then that's your choice. I don't know if he and his friend are coming, but I thought I'd let you know I'd invited him."

I had a similar conversation with my biological father the next day. Even though my parents divorced over twenty five years before, the animosity between them continued. I decided that their issues should not dictate what my relationship with each of them would look like. I genuinely wanted both of them to be at our family brunch and have the opportunity to share in our tradition.

As it turned out, neither of them attended that year. But my invitation was a monumental step for me. I was learning how not to remain entangled in unhealthy relational patterns. I could make choices and allow others to make choices as well. This was a milestone.

In previous years, I often found myself making decisions based on others' wishes, demands, or manipulations. I would obsessively try to figure out how I could please everyone and avoid causing conflict. But I was beginning to discover that God didn't hold me responsible for others' feelings, desires, or issues. He only required that I be responsible for my own and that I continue to love my family.

Sometimes we find ourselves in the middle of circumstances that have a long history attached to them. In an effort to be sensitive to all parties we may try to take on more than is required of us. I could not resolve the issues between my parents, but I could demonstrate love and honor to both of them even in the midst of their difficulties with each other. A couple years later, they both attended our Christmas brunch and spoke cordially to one another. It was a blessing to see how God worked through a simple invitation and a refusal to be entangled in issues that weren't mine to own.

What do we do when our parents and other family members are caught up in unhealthy or dysfunctional patterns? Are we required to "join in" as a sign of respect for our parents' viewpoints and opinions?

Is there a way to honor without entering into continuing family drama? Does honoring our parents mean we ignore the problematic aspects of our relationship and accept that our parents have done the "best they could"?

In the course of helping men and women deal with unhealthy relational patterns within their families, I've noticed that two essential elements always seem to come to the forefront: 1) Knowing what it looks like to be in an adult-to-adult relationship with parents and other family members; and 2) knowing how *not* to get caught in a conflict through "triangulating." Triangulating occurs when there is a conflict between two people and one person pulls in a third person to side with them.

Fostering an Adult-to-Adult Relationship

One of the most difficult transitions for families to make is the transition of a child to adulthood. Just ask anyone who's had teenagers! I remember well when my oldest daughter was sixteen. I started informally interviewing parents about how they weathered their children's adolescence. Without exception they all said essentially the same thing: "We got through it." No one said, "It was a piece of cake." These were "normal" type families who, at best, could say they'd managed to survive the transition, despite the difficulties. I felt a bit of relief knowing I wasn't alone, but I was also a bit disheartened—I was hoping to find someone who could give me that one piece of advice that would make the transition easier. We got through it too. Nothing stellar to report.

Unfortunately, some families never make that transition. Some parents try desperately to hang on to their parental authority well past their children's entrance into adulthood. Some children resist coming of age by refusing to take appropriate responsibility for themselves, failing to pursue financial independence, or sidestepping ownership of their lives and choices. When parents and children fail to transition to adult-to-adult relationships, the notion of honoring parents becomes distorted.

Honoring Dishonorable Parents

Adult children show honor not through obedience but through a respectful attitude, considerate actions, and conciliatory communication. This, of course, works best when the entire family shares a desire to transition to adult-to-adult relationships as children grow up. However, this is often not the case and therein lies the problem.

When Kyle and Ashley asked for an appointment with his parents, I knew it would be a difficult session. Kyle and Ashley had been married for about five years and Kyle's parents could not seem to accept that Kyle's focus had shifted. They repeatedly phoned Kyle or sent email messages voicing how hurt they were over their son's lack of attention. They complained that Kyle was "too involved" with his church and obviously spent more time with Ashley's parents than with them. They felt he'd purposely denied them ample time with the grandchildren and told him that other family members were upset with him for not attending all the family gatherings as he'd done in the past. Kyle's parents and family members blamed Ashley for turning Kyle against them and couldn't believe that she called herself a Christian, because in their estimation, "no good Christian would make her husband turn his back on his family."

Kyle was an emotional wreck. He'd spent most of his thirty-two years trying to appease his parents. It had only been in the previous few years that he'd come to realize that he was an adult and was now no longer responsible to obey his parents. He tried on numerous occasions to tell his parents how much he loved and appreciated them and how grateful he was to them for all the sacrifices they'd made for him, but that now as a married man and father, his priorities had changed. His parents seemed to accept his words, but their expectations and complaints continued.

When they came in for the counseling session I could feel the tension in the air. I began the session by asking Kyle's parents what their expectation was of our time together. They said they wanted to have a closer relationship with Kyle, Ashley, and their grandchildren.

I immediately noticed that whenever Kyle attempted to express himself, his mother interrupted him by expressing her views. After letting this go on a few times, I interjected my observation. Kyle's mother immediately retorted in a demeaning tone, "The boy just goes on and on about *his* family's needs and doesn't even consider how he's hurting us." I attempted to share how important it was for them as a family to respect each other and to realize that as adults they all had certain priorities for which they were responsible. I barely got my sentence out before Kyle's mother shot back, "The boy doesn't appreciate everything we've done for him," as her eyes welled up with tears. "The boy doesn't want us to see our grandchildren."

I couldn't handle it any longer. I said to Kyle's mother, "Do you realize that each time you talk about Kyle you refer to him as 'the boy'? It's going to be very important that you acknowledge that he is an adult man with his own family so that you all can move on to establish an adult-to-adult relationship with one another characterized by mutual respect."

"I've always called him 'the boy.' It's just my pet name for him. He understands what I mean," she said defensively.

There was no reasoning with her and I now understood what Kyle had faced most of his life. It amazed me that he continued to work on their relationship in spite of the unhealthy imbalance that existed. It helped explain Kyle's depression and his general defeatism as he approached life. It was clear there was no winning with mom. She had the last word, the final say, and in the end, no matter what he had to say, he was wrong.

In Kyle's case, he could not change his parents' perspective nor force his mother to acknowledge him as an adult. What he could do was speak respectfully to them *as an adult* and continue to make decisions that were consistent with his convictions as an adult, even though his parents voiced their displeasure. Over the next several months, Kyle and Ashley made repeated efforts to see his parents at sites that would be convenient for all due to the distance between their homes. But each time either

Kyle's parents didn't show up or Kyle's mother called demanding that they come to their home. Clearly, these issues did not arise the moment Kyle became an adult. These longstanding patterns only intensified once he married and was no longer under his parents' roof. Kyle seemed to be ensnared by old patterns with his parents.

As Howard M. Halpern says in *Cutting Loose*, "With our parents, we may feel at the mercy of old patterns of response that, though deeply unsatisfying, frustrating, and draining our energies, seem beyond our ability to change. We are not free and can't be free when we're still more concerned with taking care of our parents' feelings than our own and when we are still caught up in trying to win their love or avoid their displeasure."[1]

Kyle learned that he could not force his parents to acknowledge his adulthood, but he could *be* an adult who honored his parents through kindness and conciliatory efforts, even if those efforts were rejected. It was important for Kyle and Ashley to accept that their relationship with Kyle's parents was unworkable at the present time.

It was also important for Kyle to see that when we become adults we transfer the parental authority in our lives from our parents to God. It doesn't mean we forsake honoring our parents or at times seeking their advice; it does mean that as adults, we are responsible for our own decisions and are now in a parental relationship with God as our Father.

It's sometimes hard for us as parents to make that transition as well. Our children will always be our children, but once they are adults it is our responsibility to treat them as such. This means that we offer them mutual respect and offer guidance when we are asked. It means that we listen respectfully and allow them room to make their decisions without undue pressure or manipulation. We give them the freedom to be adults, to make decisions, and to take responsibility for those decisions.

Many times parents fail to recognize how hurtful it is to their adult children when they have not learned what it means to let go. The years

Don and I mentored in a young marrieds class at our church were fraught with these situations. It especially seemed to heighten around the holidays. After observing this for a while, I gave a talk entitled "Home for the Holidays." I shared some of the material I am sharing in this book. It centered on what it means to "leave and cleave" and what it looks like for couples to begin to establish their own family traditions while at the same time honoring both sets of parents.

Several couples could not believe what I was saying. They kept asking in one way or another, "Do you really mean we can make a choice for what is good for us and our kids? We don't have to run ourselves ragged making sure we please everyone?" The funny thing was most couples who struggled with these issues really *did* want to find a way to be with their respective parents on holidays. They weren't looking for a way out. They just wanted to know that their parents on both sides would be respectful of their choices and wouldn't resort to pressure tactics. I wish more parents of adult children knew that the more freedom and less guilt they impose, the better it is for all!

I'm so grateful to God that I had the opportunity to be with these couples before our oldest daughter Heather got married. It made a world of difference in how Don and I approached holiday time. Soon after Heather became engaged, the issues arose. Eric's parents divorced when he was in his early twenties and he's had little contact with his father since then. As a result, he and his sister are very close to his mother, spending every holiday with her and with their extended family. We spend most holidays with Don's family at our home or the home of one of his siblings. Don's birthday is on Christmas day so I've always done a special Christmas Eve birthday dinner with our immediate family.

I could tell early on that Heather was feeling pulled. I sat down with her and said, "Honey, we always want you to be with us, but you and Eric get to decide between the two of you what you want to do. Dad and I will never put pressure on you to be with us at the holidays. You two decide what will work best for your schedules and we'll be happy to see you whenever we can."

I have to be honest—I missed having them with us. But I'm so glad we set this up in advance. After they married, we sat them down together and repeated our commitment. We told them we love them and always look forward to having them with us, but we would respect their choice. As much as we've been able to, we have made adjustments to try to work together to allow for our different schedules and needs. This has proved to be so beneficial in our relationship. We make the most of our time and there's a freedom devoid of guilt or obligation.

Whether you are a parent with adult children or an adult child with parents still living, it is important to give the gift of respect to one another. Honoring your parents is an adult choice and a responsibility. It works best when both parents and adult children have an adult-to-adult relationship based upon mutual respect. But even if your parents don't see the relationship in the same way, you can *respond as an adult* showing honor to your parents through respectful interaction.

Next we're going to look at relational conflict and how to deal with it. Conflicts in relationship are unavoidable. Family conflicts are sometimes the most difficult because we are more vulnerable and we have more at stake. The healthy family is not defined by their lack of conflict, but by their ability to handle and resolve conflict well. We're going to discuss one pitfall in dealing with conflicts and learn a basic Scriptural principle that helps us avoid it.

Triangles Should Be Kept in Geometry Class

"Hello," I said answering the phone.

"Hi Janny, it's Dad," said the voice on the other end. It was my biological father. As the conversation ensued over the next forty five minutes, my father talked about the marital problems my sister was having and how he was upset with her for this and that; finally, he asked me what I thought. Didn't I agree with his assessment? Wouldn't it be best if my sister would do A, B, and C?" I remember offering a thought or two, but mostly I just listened to his endless frustration with my sister and her situation. I tried several times to steer the conversation in other directions without success.

I hung up the phone that day feeling sad and empty. It wasn't the first time this had happened. I couldn't figure out why I was feeling that way at first, then I realized that not once in the conversation did my dad ask about me, my husband, or his newborn grandchild—it was all about him and my sister's conflict. I wasn't clued into what I'm about to describe to you as a common pitfall in relationships, but I was aware enough of how I felt to make a stand.

I prayed and then phoned my dad back a few minutes later. I told him that I really wanted to have a relationship with him, but that it was hurtful to me that we'd spent the entire phone conversation discussing my sister's problems. I told him that it really wasn't helpful to my sister for us to talk about "what she needs to do" and that it would be better for him to have that conversation with her. I said, "Dad, for us to have a relationship it means we show interest in each other's lives. Not once in our conversation did you ask about me, Don, or your grandchild—if our conversations are always going to revolve around my sisters and their problems, then please don't call me."

What I have just described is a pattern people who are in conflict often adopt. We've all done it. It's called triangulation. When two people have a conflict with each other, one or both people try to pull in a third party to bolster their position. My dad was upset with my sister so he called me to "join" in his perspective. What often happens in these situations is that one of the two originators in the conflict takes a back seat and allows the third party in the triangle to champion their cause. The originators of the conflict are no longer talking directly to each other to try to solve the problem; the third party has now moved into a primary position, launching the attack or even becoming the target of an attack.

How does this happen? Take the example of my dad and sister. After the one-sided conversation described above, he initiates a call to my sister and "casually" mentions that I feel exactly the same way he does about her marriage problems. He is quick to point out that I think he is "right" and since "we" see it the same way my sister is obviously wrong if she doesn't take what we have determined to be her best course of action. That conversation ends abruptly, followed by a phone call from my sister to me. In addition to remaining angry at my dad for his insensitivity to her situation, she is furious with me for "taking his side."

Triangulation reflects a failure to resolve a conflict between two persons. The third person has no business in the conflict but is pulled in to provide validation for one side or the other. This often derails the conflict resolution from taking place between the two persons because they continue to avoid dealing directly with each other. Furthermore, the people who get caught up in the triangulation often don't know what hit them. They never intended to choose a side—they were simply listening and making comments but had no intention of joining the fray.

There are two ways that you avoid triangulation in a conflict. The first is simple. When you and another person have a conflict with each other, you refuse to take that conflict to anyone else but the person with whom you have conflict. This isn't to say that, at times, you may need assistance if all your attempts to resolve the conflict have been unsuccessful. But it *does* mean that you don't call another friend to talk about the issue in an attempt to "build your case" or gain their support. It means you follow what Scripture says in Matthew 18:15: "If your brother or sister sins, go and point out their fault, just between the two of you. If they listen to you, you have won them over" (NIV).

Jesus instructs us to 1) deal directly with the person who has hurt us and 2) take the initiative. Elsewhere in Scripture we're told that the resolution of relational conflict is so important to God that we are to reconcile with a brother who "has something against [us]" even before we offer our gifts to God (Matthew 5:23 NIV).

There are times that you may find it necessary to talk to another person outside of the conflict just to gain some perspective. But this person must have the ability to avoid simply taking up your cause. Obtaining genuine feedback from others includes asking them things like: *How could I have handled this differently? Do you think I'm being unreasonable in my expectations? Are there ways to approach this conversation with my friend that you think would be helpful?* Notice that the feedback you ask for is focused not on the other person, but on you. When you've done that, you incorporate that valuable information back into your conversation with the person with whom you have the conflict and work toward a resolution.

So, the first way you avoid triangulation is you determine to speak directly to the person with whom you have a conflict or misunderstanding and remain committed to working together to resolve it.

The second way you avoid the snare of triangulation is to refuse the invitation to join in the conflict. For some people this is very difficult. Imagine this scenario:

Your recently widowed mother calls you about how lonely she's feeling. You live fifteen hundred miles away and you have a brother who lives in her same town. She talks about how your brother doesn't seem to understand her need for conversation. She shares how grateful she is that he's always available to do projects around the house for her like trim the roses, install a new lock, or replace a light bulb, but he never has time to sit down and visit with her. As you're listening you are feeling for your mother. She's not lived by herself for over fifty years and she and your father were very close. You feel bad that you don't live closer. You start to feel a little bit of frustration with your brother even though you can appreciate the fact that he has a demanding job and a family. You want to validate your mom's feelings *and* you want your brother to understand what she's going through and find time to spend more time with her. What do you do?

You have a couple options:

The common response: You tell your mother how sorry you are that she is lonely and that you understand how hard it must be for her to be alone in her house without your dad. You try to reassure her and encourage her to connect with her friends at the church and just allow herself some time to grieve. You say that you appreciate your brother's efforts to help her, but you agree that he should not just focus on the household projects. He should be spending more time sitting down with her, having dinner with her once or twice a week, and allowing her to cry on his shoulder. You say to your mother, "I wish I were there so I could do those things for you." Your mother starts to cry and says, "I wish you were here too." You hang up feeling sad, guilty, and little angry with your brother. You tell yourself that your brother has never really been that compassionate and that he needs to be more understanding. You decide your brother needs to know these things and you call him immediately.

Or a healthier response: You tell your mother how sorry you are that she is lonely and that you understand how hard it must be after all these years to be alone in her house without your dad. You listen to her and try to reassure her. You tell her this will take some time, but that it's important that she connect with her friends at church and when she's ready, perhaps attend the grief group offered there. Then you say that it sounds like she appreciates your brother's efforts around her house, but you hear that she'd like more connection with him. You say to your mother, "Mom, it's okay for you to talk to him about this. Next time he's over ask him to come sit with you in the family room so you can chat for a few minutes." Mom may resist this idea at first. "No, I don't want to make him feel bad—he already does so much for me." "Mom, Steven is doing a lot for you, but I think he would like to know from you what is really important to you. Why don't you tell him what you've told me, that you appreciate all he does for you, but from time to time you just want him to sit down with you and visit awhile? I think you'd feel better just being able to tell him and I'm sure he'd appreciate hearing that from you."

You can see from the second scenario that refusing the invitation to join in or to get "triangulated" doesn't mean that you lack compassion or empathy. It simply means that you do not take up someone else's cause and that you encourage them to deal directly with the person themselves.

In my family, this has not been easy. Boundaries have not always been respected and it has been difficult to navigate relationships with many of my family members who are used to being enmeshed in other's issues. But I have learned that although I can't change them or make them value healthy communication, I can be responsible for myself and not get pulled into the drama when it occurs.

Triangulation is a common problem in relationships of all kinds. It happens in our families, in our churches, in our workplace. We may not be able to influence others not to triangulate, but we can make a choice not to invite others into our conflicts and decline the invitation by others to join theirs.

In summary, there are two very important aspects of not becoming entangled in unhealthy relational patterns: knowing what it means to be in an adult-to-adult relationship with our parents and avoiding triangulation when there is a conflict within the family. Avoiding these two common pitfalls enables us to honor our parents even when unhealthy relational patterns exist. There are certainly additional topics that could be addressed here. There are others who have dealt more extensively with some of these issues in their books which I've listed in the appendix.

Chapter 5

HONORING DOESN'T MEAN BEING OVERLY-RESPONSIBLE

"Does honoring your parents mean that you should always be available to help them when they're in need?" Terri asked from the audience.

"Not necessarily," I said, "Can you tell me a little more?"

"Well," she said with a sigh, "my mother is in jail again for stealing and she is begging me to post bail and have her released into my custody."

"Terri, you said your mother is in jail *again*. Does she have a history of this sort of behavior?"

"Yes, I'm afraid so. She's been arrested multiple times, evicted from every apartment she's lived in, and has even stolen from me when I've allowed her to stay in our home. The last time she lived with us, I told her it was the last time because I'm concerned about my children and the influence she is having on them. My husband and I have spent thousands of dollars helping her out over the years and to be honest, I don't want to bail her out. But I'm feeling guilty. I want to honor my mom, but I'm not sure what that looks like."

This scenario may not be typical; however, there are some important principles that can be drawn from Terri's predicament. What do we do when one or both of our parents request our help or intervention? Is it unloving or dishonoring to refuse to give them assistance or aid? How do we avoid crossing the line between helping them and inappropriately enabling their behavior?

Owning the Problem

Early in our marriage Don and I faced some tough decisions concerning Don's father. His alcoholism made it difficult for him to hold down a job, and while he'd had periods of sobriety, they'd been short-lived. It was clear that outside intervention would be necessary.

When we had been married less than a year, Don's father called us asking if we would take him to the hospital for treatment. Since Don's mother didn't drive, he needed our assistance. It happened to be Labor Day so we spent our day off sitting with him in the emergency room until he was finally admitted. I was very hopeful that this would be the turning point. He spent a couple weeks in the hospital receiving medical treatment and attending alcohol abuse meetings. By the time he was released his color was back from the ashen gray, he'd gained a little weight, and he said he was ready to look for a job and get back to work. But it became clear almost immediately that he had no intention of attending AA or even admitting that he had an alcohol problem.

As a matter of fact, despite intermittent detoxes over subsequent years, Don's father wouldn't admit he was an alcoholic. After each hospitalization his intentions were good, but he refused to attend meetings, insisting he "wasn't like those people at AA."

Don and I wanted to ask the family to participate in an intervention, but it became clear early on that other family members, and most importantly Don's mother, were not on board with this approach. As is true in many alcoholic homes, the spouse and family members were deeply entrenched as codependents of the alcoholic. Don's mother didn't get help for herself, and family members continued to enable his father's drinking. We were at a loss as to how to intervene in a productive, supportive manner.

His father's drinking pattern was predictable. He would be sober for three months, followed by a binge that could last for several months. His health would decline and he would call one of the seven kids to take him to the hospital for treatment. After observing this endless non-productive pattern, Don and I decided we could not participate. We continued to love and pray for Don's dad and participate in family gatherings, but we were unwilling to transport him to the hospital to be detoxed until we saw some significant indication that he had owned his alcohol problem.

Unfortunately, that day never came. In the final year of Don's father's life he was not drinking but he essentially lost all his dignity and the affection of his children. Everyone had tired of offering help and most had little contact with him, to his utter dismay. I'm so grateful that we were able to share God's love with him two weeks before his passing and we were assured of his salvation prior to his death.

Honoring your parents need not entail rescuing or enabling them. But it can be difficult to discern the difference between helping or assisting on one hand, and enabling or rescuing on the other. "Enabling is doing something for someone, that they could, and should be doing themselves."[1] Enabling can also mean contributing in some way to helping a person continue in a lifestyle that is harmful or unproductive. This may take the form of financial rescuing, calling a boss and making excuses on a person's behalf, contributing to a person's irresponsible behavior through rationalizing or blaming others, circumventing natural consequences for a person's behavior, trying to control or fix a person and their problems, or repeatedly giving a person "one more chance." In essence, we enable when we own their problem as our own, rather than requiring a person to take responsibility for their own life and issues.

This becomes especially complicated when dealing with parents, as in Terry's case with her mother who was in and out of jail and had "no one else" to turn to. One way to evaluate whether our actions are helpful or enabling is to ask ourselves some questions:
- Are my actions helping the other person grow in maturity? (i.e., taking responsibility for themselves and their problem/issue) or are my actions promoting more irresponsibility and dependence?
- Are my actions contributing to a long-standing problem that has not been faced in truth?
- Are my actions circumventing some natural consequences?
- Is my intervention causing this person to depend on me rather than on God?
- Do I feel frustrated, taken advantage of, resentful, or unappreciated when offering help or intervention?
- Are there indications from others that my actions are perpetuating the problem?

Sometimes it is helpful to run through these questions with the help of someone who can be objective about the issues at hand. Preferably it should be someone who is not directly in relationship with the person and someone who understands what it means to have healthy boundaries.

We cannot measure the helpfulness of our actions by the response of the person we are helping. They have a vested interest in receiving the kind of help that allows them to continue in their own irresponsibility. Like most of us, they like the status quo; they may resist or reject any help that brings disequilibrium and discomfort.

Over-Responsibility: A Case Study

Nita, a young woman in her thirties came to counseling for help in dealing with her parents. Her parents immigrated to the United States from Asia when she was a small child. Nita and her three sisters were educated in the States, but she was finding it difficult to determine what honoring her parents meant in light of traditional cultural mandates. She explained that it is customary in the Korean culture for the eldest son to care for the parents in their aging years. However, since she had no male siblings, the responsibility had been delegated to her. She had put herself through college and was working as a professional with a well-paying job. In keeping with Korean custom, she lived at home since she was still unmarried. But she also had just recently become engaged, and this had led indirectly to some family conflict revolving around financial matters.

Nita filled me in on some pertinent family history. Several years previously her father made some very poor financial investments that resulted in near bankruptcy. Nita, who had been saving for her future, was the only one of the children who had significant resources. She ended up giving her parents $25,000 to help them with their financial situation. Her parents were extremely grateful and promised to repay her when their situation improved, but her father's business only took in a meager income—just enough to provide for the family's food and shelter. Furthermore, since Nita was living at home, she contributed $1200 monthly to help offset expenses.

After becoming engaged, Nita spoke with her parents about discontinuing her monthly contribution in order to pay for her wedding, which was her sole responsibility. Her mother became very upset with her request, making excuses about how this would put "too much stress upon the family." Later, Nita learned that her parents were giving most of her rent money to her older sister whose husband refused to work. She also learned that her father continued to make unwise business decisions that were perpetuating their financial instability.

Nita had mixed feelings. She felt angry that her hard-earned money had been doled out to her sister's family without her knowledge and she felt pressured to continue to lend financial support to her sister's family, primarily because of her nephews. She felt bad for her father who worked very hard but carried tremendous shame over his business failures. Her mother particularly played upon her guilt. She would tell Nita that God had blessed her with a good job and that she should "honor" them for the sacrifices they'd made in bringing the family to the United States. Nita needed help sorting out what her responsibility was to her aging parents.

Let's ask some of the questions that were presented earlier:

- Are Nita's actions helping her father and brother-in-law grow in maturity? Are these two family members taking appropriate responsibility for themselves, their families, and their business decisions?

No. Nita's financial contribution is enabling her father to avoid the issues of poor money management and unwise business decisions. It is also contributing to her brother-in-law's refusal to take the appropriate responsibility to care and provide for his family.

- Are Nita's actions promoting more irresponsibility and dependence?

Yes. Neither her father nor her brother-in-law are actively pursuing avenues that would allow them to grow in the areas in which they are irresponsible. They are willing to be recipients, but they are not seeking change and accountability.

- Are Nita's actions contributing to a longstanding problem that has not been faced in truth?

Yes. Her father's past and most recent business decisions reflect a pattern that he has not humbly faced. He feels shame over his failures, but he has not sought wisdom or counsel from others and continues to make poor decisions because he is trying to correct his behavior in isolation. Her brother-in-law is not dealing in a godly manner with a reality of life. "If anyone will not work, neither shall he eat" (2 Thessalonians 3:10b NKJV).

- Are Nita's actions circumventing some natural consequences?

Yes. In both circumstances the natural consequences are being interrupted.

- Is Nita's intervention causing this person to depend on her rather than on God?

This may be hard to evaluate in a given situation. One question that I might ask a client is: Is your intervention contributing to the person's overall dependence on God, as evidenced by their pursuit of God's guidance and instruction, or is it causing the person to look to you as the solution to their problem? If the latter is truer than the former, then you are putting yourself in the place of God. The Bible calls this idolatry. God will not share that position with anyone or anything.

Another way to evaluate whether our "helping" is creating dependence on us rather than on God is by observing the response of the one being helped. If you suggest the possibility of discontinuing your help, you will most likely get an immature response from the person who is looking to you rather than God. It may come in the form of anger, blaming, guilt-manipulation, depression, or self-pity. A person who is looking to God as their primary source will accept your decision respectfully and express gratitude for what you provided up to that point. They may have uncertainty and concern over the future, but they will not overly burden you with those concerns.

In Nita's case, as we discussed these questions thoroughly, it became quite clear to her that through her "helping" she was actually interfering with the work she sensed God wanted to do in her father's heart and life. She had seen many times that her father's shame kept him from being truly honest and vulnerable with good, godly men who surrounded him.

She could see that "helping" her father had actually inhibited the process. With her sister and brother-in-law, she sensed that she was in the middle of their marital relationship because she was allowing her sister to depend upon her rather than seek God.

- Does Nita feel frustrated, taken advantage of, resentful, or unappreciated when offering help or intervention?

Yes. Nita felt all of the above, but felt guilty for feeling as she did. We had to work on boundaries to help her distinguish between her responsibilities and the responsibilities of others. Part of her struggle was she did not want anyone in her family to be angry with her. I reminded her that those who were angry with her for setting appropriate boundaries were the ones with the problem. Appropriate boundaries offer others the opportunity to look at areas in their own lives that need healing and change. Nita further discovered that she was not only investing herself financially, but she was also expending more time and emotional energy on their problems than they were.

- Are there indications from others that Nita's actions are contributing to the perpetuation of the problem?

Yes. One of Nita's sisters supported her in discontinuing paying rent. She reminded Nita of several instances over the years where her parents could have paid back a portion of the $25,000 she had given them, but instead chose to travel back to Asia or give a gift to the church so as to appear generous.

Nita was able to withdraw her financial support gradually while maintaining a loving, supportive posture toward her parents. It was an adjustment for everyone to begin to move toward a healthier adult-to-adult relationship. Even though her father's business situation did not improve, nor did her brother-in-law rush out to get a job, Nita was able to care for family members without taking on the responsibility of their well-being. She was beginning the process of leaving her father and mother and laying the groundwork for cleaving to her husband.

Step In or Sit This One Out?

I felt overly responsible for my mother's emotional well-being after my stepfather died. I was her emotional support while I was growing up, so it was a very familiar feeling. My mother was my stepfather's sole caretaker for several years after he was diagnosed with dementia. She could not bear to place him in a nursing home even though she was emotionally and physically exhausted trying to care for him. For several years, they had not attended church or had any social outlets. My mother's life was consumed with my stepfather's care. Only when he fell and broke his hip a month before he died did she finally place him in nursing facility near her home. She spent every day there, supervising his care and remaining at his side until just before dark.

After his death she was devastated and lonely. As is true of many caregivers, her own health had deteriorated due to exhaustion. Even though I made several trips up to see her after my stepfather's death it did little to quell her loneliness. Our daily phone conversations often included comments about her "wishing I lived closer" and ended in tearful goodbyes.

The mobile home park where they lived had an excellent reputation for being a safe, supportive community for seniors that offered activities and classes. But whenever I encouraged my mother to participate in bingo or attend a themed dinner in the recreation hall, she would list all the reasons why she couldn't go. I knew that it would not be helpful for me to spend extended periods of time with her in her home even though she expressed her loneliness daily. Eventually, I encouraged her to join a grief group so she could be with others who were also learning to adjust to life on their own. The grief group proved to be just what she needed. She began making new friends and she met others who were in their own grief process.

Gradually my mother started connecting with neighbors and accepting invitations to luncheons and other activities in the mobile home park. Today, six years after my stepfather's death, she has multiple friends and attends functions as her health permits. She attends an exercise class for seniors, goes to bingo most Monday nights, and hosts a Canasta group in her home once a month.

You may be asking yourself if you are over-responsible or appropriately helpful in your relationship with your parents. If you're single, share with some of your friends about your situation. How do they react? If you're married, ask your spouse about your involvement with your parents. Is your spouse supportive or think you're in over your head? For some of us, being over-responsible seems to be hard-wired into us. We automatically tend to take on more than is ours to bear. We need others in our lives who can provide more objective feedback. And, we need to take heed.

Listen to what Galatians 6:2–5 says:

Carry each other's burdens, and in this way you will fulfill the law of Christ. If anyone thinks they are something when they are not, they deceive themselves. Each one should test their own actions. Then they can take pride in themselves alone, without comparing themselves to someone else, for each one should carry their own load. (NIV)

Do you hear both the collective and personal responsibility in these verses? Do you hear any conflict here between "carrying each other's burdens" and "each one should carry his own load"? It's important to look at the original Greek words that are used here. The Greek word for *burdens* refers to "oppressive burdens" and it highlights the necessity of care and support within the Christian community.[2] The Greek word for *load* means "weight or burden of responsibility." Each person bears responsibility for his own actions and the tasks assigned to him or her.[3]

In other words, we are to help those who are experiencing hardship due to heavy or oppressive burdens. But we are not responsible to relieve capable individuals of their personal responsibilities. I once heard Dr. Henry Cloud say that the *burden* is like a huge boulder that is too large for us to carry alone; it could crush us. We need the help of others to carry those kinds of burdens. But the *load* he likens to a knapsack that we are expected to carry on our own. These are the things we're individually responsible for like our own feelings, attitudes, and behaviors.

Honor doesn't mean we are to be over-responsible with our parents. We are to carry our own load and allow them to do the same.

Chapter 6

HONORING DOESN'T MEAN IGNORING ILLEGAL, IMMORAL, OR TOXIC BEHAVIOR

Cindy was in a quandary. She called me out of the blue one afternoon and I could hear the distress in her voice. Cindy was a former sexual abuse support group member whom I had not spoken with in several years.

"What's going on, Cindy?" I asked.

"Jan, I just learned from my thirteen-year-old daughter that my father sexually abused her when she was six. I could hardly believe it but when she told me the details I knew it was true. There were so many similarities with what he'd done to me as a child."

We talked for nearly an hour as Cindy related the details of her daughter's disclosure and what had been done subsequently. Cindy recounted how hard she had worked in the support group to deal with her own abuse and ultimately forgive her father. They had restored their relationship, but now she was at a crossroads. The abuse was reported to the authorities and an investigation was being conducted. She hated that her daughter had to undergo all the questioning and repeat details that were so familiar. It brought back forgotten feelings that she thought she'd resolved.

Her dilemma was whether or not she should pursue further legal action. Should she put her daughter through the legal process of going to court and telling her story? How would other family members react if they pursued legal action? Was this the right thing to do as a Christian? Had she *really* forgiven her father for what he'd done to her or was she using this situation finally to get her own justice?

I asked Cindy what was most important to her. Without hesitation she said, "I just want my dad to get some help. I want him to go to counseling so he can get to the root of this in his own life. I really need God's wisdom right now."

How does honor work in a situation like this? Is it possible to pursue legal action against one's parent and maintain honor at the same time? Isn't it better *not* to bring such issues into the legal arena but try to deal with them in the context of the family or community of believers? What, if anything, does Scripture have to say about illegal behavior? What about immoral behavior on the part of a parent? How does one honor a parent whose behavior is immoral in the eyes of God? Does honor mean we ignore the behavior? What do we do with parents who are difficult or toxic in their communication with us? Do we ignore it and just do our best to love them in spite of how it injures us?

These issues cannot be resolved with a "one size fits all" approach. There are individual circumstances that must be prayerfully considered and outcomes that must be weighed. There are some biblical principles that can serve as a foundational guide, but individuals whose parents are involved in illegal, immoral, or toxic behavior should seek counsel from professionals as well as pastors in order to apply God's wisdom in their specific situation.

The Bible does have something to say to us regarding what to expect when we've crossed the line by doing wrong:

> Consequently, whoever rebels against the authority is rebelling against what God has instituted, and those who do so will bring judgment on themselves. For rulers hold no terror for those who do right, but for those who do wrong. Do you want to be free from fear of the one in authority? Then do what is right and you will be commended. For the one in authority is God's servant for your good. But if you do wrong, be afraid, for rulers do not bear the sword for no reason. They are God's servant, agents of wrath to bring punishment on the wrongdoer. (Romans 13:2–4 NIV)

God seems to be saying here that there is a cause and effect principle. If we do something wrong in the eyes of the law, we should expect consequences.

Sometimes God uses the law to teach us because we refuse to learn any other way. In their book *Boundaries*, Drs. Cloud and Townsend say it this way:

> The law of cause and effect is a basic law of life. The Bible calls it the Law of Sowing and Reaping. *When God tells us that we will reap what we sow, he is not punishing us; he's telling us how things really are.*[1]

The authors go on to say that sometimes the Law of Sowing and Reaping is interrupted because someone steps in to circumvent the natural consequences of another's actions. When this happens, the "rescuer" enables the person to continue in their irresponsible or wrong behavior. By doing so, the "wrongdoer" does not experience the benefit of reaping what they've sown. We see how this principle works throughout the scriptures and how God allows this reaping and sowing in order to bring about true repentance and change in the heart of the wrongdoer.

In Cindy's situation there were several things to consider. First and foremost were her daughter's needs. How was Cindy to demonstrate care and protection for her? What might the ramifications be should she decide not to press charges? What message might she be sending her daughter about the offenses she'd suffered from her grandfather? If she did pursue legal action, would the legal process inflict further emotional trauma to her daughter? Since her father confessed to his wrongdoing, wasn't that sufficient? What should relationship look like with her father now and in the future? We discussed several of these questions together and I prayed with Cindy at the end of our conversation. She wanted to gather more information from the district attorney and talk more with her father and other family members before she made a decision.

Several months later Cindy called to tell me what had transpired. After our conversation, she approached her father who seemed genuinely repentant over his actions. She told him that she was willing to forgive him, but there would be some necessary boundaries in place to insure the protection of her daughter. She told him that he must be in counseling if they were ever to resume any semblance of relationship. She emphasized his need to deal with the roots of his behavior that led to abusing both her and her daughter. Her father refused, saying that God had forgiven him and that there was no need for counseling.

Cindy said, "When I heard that, I knew what I had to do." She said it became very clear that she must pursue legal action on behalf of her daughter, as well as others who might be in danger in the future. She obtained counseling for her daughter, which helped in the process of the trial that followed. As a result, her father was sent to jail for a period of time, he was not allowed to have contact with any minor children, and was required by the court to attend counseling while on probation for five years. Cindy said it was a difficult decision, but she knew that in the long run it was best for all concerned.

"At least he's going to counseling and he has the opportunity to gain some insight into his behavior. That's really all that I wanted in the first place. I think the added benefit was that my daughter knew that her mom would stand up and fight to protect her. I never got that from my own mom, but I'm glad I could do it for my daughter."

Cindy's response to her father's actions *kept her father from acting dishonorably* toward her daughter and other children. I wonder if setting boundaries or pursuing legal action in certain circumstances can be a way of showing honor to a parent who would act dishonorably were those limitations not imposed. It's something to consider.

Nature versus Nurture

When my husband and I taught an engaged couples class at our church, we encountered an all too common issue. It had to do with a couple's wedding. One young bride I spoke with was devastated as she planned her wedding. Krista shared how her parents had divorced when she was four. Her biological father was a drug addict and had been in and out of jail since before she was born. Her mother remarried when she was eight and her stepfather assumed all financial responsibility for her and her sisters. He was her softball coach, paid for her braces, and helped pay for her college education. Krista's paternal grandparents played a big role in her life and were themselves very distraught over their son's drug usage over the years. They maintained involvement in Krista's life, attending school plays, sporting events, and graduation ceremonies—even though their son, Krista's father, was uninvolved and disinterested.

When Krista became engaged, her grandparents were excited for her. As she began preparing for the wedding, which was financed by her mother and stepfather, the issue of who would walk her down the aisle came to the forefront. There was no doubt in Krista's mind that her stepfather would have the privilege, but her grandparents took exception to her decision. They were so upset that Krista was not asking her father to do so that they refused to attend the wedding and cut off all communication with her. Krista was distraught. Were her grandparents right in saying she was dishonoring them and her biological father by asking her stepfather to escort her down the aisle? Was she supposed to give her father another chance even though he'd been through multiple rehab programs only to continue in his addiction? Was she required to give this honor to her father even though they had no relationship and he'd made few efforts to connect with her over the years?

When the Bible talks about honoring our parents, it is referring to the person(s) that actually did the parenting, not just those who gave us birth.[2] You may choose to honor uninvolved biological parents in various ways such as inviting them to a wedding ceremony, acknowledging them on Mother's Day, or periodically sending pictures or updates of your family. But you are not dishonoring your parents if you don't.

Immoral Behavior

What about immoral behavior? How does one deal with a parent who committed adultery? What about a mother who has multiple live-in boyfriends? What about a father who repeatedly cheats on your mother? Does honor require that an adult child ignore or downplay such actions for the sake of "keeping the peace" in the relationship?

Tyler knew about his father's womanizing and involvement with pornography from the time he was a teenager. His mother had done her best to keep things from her four children, but Tyler put two and two together. His parents stayed together until he was twenty eight, when his mother's discovery of yet another marital affair ended the marriage. His father married the woman with whom he'd had the affair and Tyler had no idea how he should navigate his relationship with his parents. His mother felt betrayed when Tyler mentioned contact with his father and his new wife. Tyler also struggled with his own feelings of anger toward his father for his philandering over the years. He found it difficult to honor his father when his father had acted so dishonorably toward his mother and his siblings over the years. What does honor look like in these circumstances?

First of all, it's important to state that people can honor their parents without feeling compelled to accept their lifestyle or remaining in ongoing relationships with them. In Tyler's situation, it would be completely understandable and even advisable for him to take some time to work through his own feelings about his father's betrayal, which was not limited to his mother only, but to him as a son. It would be extremely beneficial for him to obtain some help in the form of a support group, individual counseling, or pastoral counseling where he could work through his anger and disillusionment, and obtain wise counsel about what a future relationship with his father might entail. Any future relationship would have to be based on his father's acceptance of responsibility for his past behavior. If Tyler's father refuses to "own" his behavior as wrong and maintains a position of excusing himself or blaming his ex-wife, then Tyler may decide to end contact altogether.

If Tyler resumes relationship with his father it will be important for him to be able to talk to his father adult to adult about how his father's behavior impacted him. He must not assume responsibility to speak for his mother or his siblings, but simply himself. He may need to tell his father that he needs time alone with him before he is able to enter into relationship with his father's new wife. He will probably have to be clear about what his father can expect from him during the holidays and what the relationship will probably look like with his father's new wife, at least initially.

Tyler will need to find what works best for him and be as open in his communication as possible. Some of Tyler's decisions about the relationship with his father will depend upon his father's response. If his father is unwilling to accept Tyler's needs or becomes defensive concerning his past behavior, Tyler may have to explain to his father that a separation season seems to be in order.

This raises a question: Is it possible to honor a parent while having little or no contact with him or her? As mentioned earlier in the chapter on "not subjecting yourself or your children to harm," temporary separation may be necessary in order to enter into a "season of healing." We also talked about setting boundaries in our relationships with parents when there is a need to protect ourselves or our children from harm. There are other times we may take a timeout or set some necessary boundaries for the sake *of the relationship*—not simply for protection *from the relationship*.

Boundaries that Preserve

Sometimes I learn things the hard way. Just ask my husband. It took me years in my relationship with my biological father to learn this simple concept: boundaries work to *preserve relationships* as well as protect us from harm.

Early in our marriage, I hung up the phone in tears again. My husband Don made an astute observation: "Honey, every time you talk with your father it seems to upset you. He baits you into discussing subjects that are destined for controversy. Why don't you stop taking the bait?"

I knew he was right, but what could I do? As I recalled various conversations with my dad over the years, they all seemed to start off fine. We exchanged greetings, caught up on family news, and discussed his travel plans. Then it hit me. Usually about ten minutes into the conversation, my dad would start talking about his investments, money issues, televangelists, or some other religious group or organization that he thought was bogus. He would invariably ask me what I thought and then proceed to shred my opinion, leaving me wondering what in the world had happened. Or he would deride all Christians as hypocrites and liars who were bilking old ladies out of their money and making outrageous unverifiable claims of healing and miracles.

I would step into the "trap" repeatedly and my dad seemed to revel in the controversial conversation that would ensue. I am embarrassed to tell you how long this went on before I came upon a very simple solution. As I reflected on how our conversation was quite peaceable for the first ten minutes I decided to try a little experiment over the next few months. When my dad called or when I phoned him, I would set my kitchen timer to ten minutes. When the buzzer went off, I would politely say, "Dad, I'm going to have to go now, but it was nice catching up with you. Glad to hear you're feeling well and continuing to square dance. Take care of yourself. I'll talk to you soon."

The first few times, I felt guilty because the conversation was short and shallow. But soon, I realized that the conversations were quite pleasant in nature and I hung up feeling good rather than beaten down. I used the buzzer for several months just to help me establish a new pattern. I wondered if my dad heard the buzzer in the background. He never mentioned it, nor did I. I chuckled a little as I thought maybe my dad wondered why I was always in the kitchen baking when we talked on the phone!

I maintain time-limited phone conversations with my dad even now (he is ninety five). Our relationship is cordial and it remains on a surface level, but these self-imposed boundaries have helped temper the antagonism that previously characterized our conversations. I no longer use the buzzer but I have an internal "alert" that goes off inside when it's time to bring the conversation to a close.

"Boundaries are *not* rejections," writes Mark Sichel in his book *Healing from Family Rifts*. "They are, in fact, ways to live harmoniously with other people in mutual respect."[3]

This simple solution really helped to preserve a relationship that has been a difficult one for most of my adult life. I'm thankful that God has supplied the grace I needed to show honor, care, and concern for my biological father while maintaining personal boundaries that helped to preserve peace in the relationship rather than allowing it to be destroyed. I am so grateful to God for all that He continues to teach me in this process. I am learning how to let go of unmet needs from my father so that I might open myself up fully to the loving embrace of my only true Father.

Boundaries that Protect

Jocelyn was a thirty-year-old pastor's wife whom I met at a retreat. She was a beautiful, petite woman with a gentle spirit and an infectious smile. To look at her you would have thought she had no cares in the world. As we sat down one afternoon to chat, tears formed in her eyes as she told the following story.

She married her husband Brian five years previously after they had graduated from college and were working at a nonprofit ministry. They'd fallen deeply in love and desired to serve God together. When Jocelyn first introduced Brian to her parents they were thrilled. During their courtship they talked about Brian attending seminary, which would have required moving from their home state. When they followed this course of action, both sets of parents were initially supportive, but in the years following, her parents became increasingly discontent. They sent several emails a week requesting that she come home for a visit by herself so they could reconnect.

As I listened, I thought it was a classic case of parents who missed their daughter and were grieving over their loss of connection.

"So, your parents miss you and want to see you," I said.

"Yes, that's true. But I'm afraid there is more to it than that," Jocelyn said through tears. "My parents have specifically asked that I come alone. They don't want Brian to come with me and I'm not sure what to do."

"Are your parents upset because of the move? Or is there more to it than that?" I asked.

Jocelyn unfolded more of her story. The issues seemed to arise early in her relationship with Brian. Jocelyn was the oldest child of four and was extremely close to her mother. When Brian entered the picture, Jocelyn's mother felt threatened by their relationship and tried subtle tactics to persuade Jocelyn not to pursue the relationship with Brian.

Once they were engaged and it became clear that Jocelyn was making the shift of leaving her parents and cleaving to her husband, her mother pulled out the heavy artillery. Her mother's anger and guilt-manipulation was expressed in phone calls and multiple emails that said things like, "You've changed; you're not our same daughter anymore." Her mother told her how ashamed she was of her, and that according to their family doctor, *she* was the cause of her grandfather's recent stroke. She said Jocelyn was dishonoring both her parents and grandparents and was treating them horribly by not agreeing to meet with her parents alone.

Jocelyn was attempting to deal with her parents adult to adult, but her mom couldn't seem to make the transition. She was accustomed to Jocelyn buckling under her pressure and now her mom was making it a power struggle. Jocelyn felt torn. She wanted to maintain closeness with her family but also wanted to honor her husband, their marriage, and what she believed Scripture teaches. Unfortunately, for some families this is a nearly impossible transition. It is sometimes difficult to apply the same sound principles to our families that we would apply in other relationships.

A good test of your relationship with your parents, or anyone for that matter, is whether or not they love your "no" as much as they love your "yes." If we find ourselves in relationships with people who only love our compliance we may need to look closely at the value of such a relationship. We know we've transitioned to a healthy adult-to-adult relationship with our parents and others when there is a mutual respect for each others' choices.

Jocelyn said she and Brian sat down together and responded to each email in careful consideration of the feelings of her parents and family, but each attempt to bridge the relationship was met with resistance and insistence that Jocelyn come home and meet with her parents without Brian.

"We even offered to fly back home to meet with a counselor who could help us sort out the issues. But to date, they've refused. I don't know what else to do. I feel so caught in the middle."

The more Jocelyn talked, the more the picture became clear. Jocelyn's mother couldn't handle her lack of control in Jocelyn's life. She had always been able to intimidate and persuade Jocelyn by using guilt tactics and pressure, but this wasn't working. When Brian entered the picture and was not intimidated by his mother-in-law's demands, the status quo was disrupted. It was also evident from her mom's emails that she wasn't clear about what it means to honor your parents as an adult. She told Jocelyn that God demands that children honor and obey their parents, and that they didn't stop being her parents just because she was married.

Jocelyn was distraught and exhausted. It didn't matter how she responded to her mother's emails; her words were misunderstood and discredited. It seemed as though reconciliation was impossible.

My first recommendation to Jocelyn was to stop responding to the emails as it was causing more hurt and adding fuel to the fire. I encouraged her to draft a final email stating her and Brian's desire for reconciliation and their willingness to meet in person all together. In it she made it clear that sending more emails back and forth was not going to bring about any resolution or restoration. She communicated her love to her parents and simply asked that they all have mutual respect for one another's marriages and families. She affirmed that she would always be their daughter, but as a thirty-year-old adult married woman, her highest priorities were to God and her husband. She closed her email expressing her love along with a genuine request that they meet. Jocelyn did what Drs. Cloud and Townsend recommend in their book *The Mom Factor*—she gave herself permission to be an adult and to relate to her mother as an equal.[4]

It has been over three years since Jocelyn wrote to them and there has been no response from her parents regarding willingness to meet with them as a couple. Her mother still sends messages through other family members that seem to indicate there has been little change. It was going to be mom's way or no way. Jocelyn still carries sadness over the loss of the relationship, but she is at peace over her attempts to bring a healthy resolution. Jocelyn did her part by loving her mom while maintaining her adulthood and protecting the unity of her marriage.

If you've been struggling with your relationship with a parent who has acted illegally, immorally, or one who is difficult or toxic in their dealings with you, it's my prayer that you will ask God to help you navigate through it and to discern what it is that he wants to do in your heart in the process.

As you have seen from the examples in this chapter, we often need the objectivity of someone outside the family system to help us in these kinds of situations. We've seen through the case of Cindy and her father that honoring doesn't mean sweeping illegal behavior under the rug. Honor doesn't mean that we are bound by biological ties when there is an absence of relational connection, as was the case with Krista and her biological father. Tyler's situation taught us that honor doesn't mean disregarding a parent's moral failure just to keep the peace. Finally, honor doesn't mean we can't set appropriate boundaries with a difficult or toxic parent in order to preserve the relationship as in Jocelyn's situation and in my relationship with my father. It may seem counter-intuitive, but sometimes setting boundaries is the healthiest way to honor a parent.

We've spent the last six chapters discussing what honor doesn't mean. We learned that as adults we are not bound to the requirement of always pleasing our parents. We are not obligated to pretend that bad things did not happen in our families. Honor doesn't mean subjecting ourselves or our children to parents' harmful behavior or becoming entangled in unhealthy relational patterns such as triangulating. Honor doesn't mean that we are to be overly-responsible for our parents by rescuing or enabling them. And finally, we should never ignore a parent's behavior that is illegal, immoral, or toxic.

Now that you have seen some examples of what honor doesn't mean, let's look at what honor *does* mean from a biblical perspective and how Jesus exemplified honoring His earthly parents.

SECTION II

WHAT HONOR MEANS

I sat down with my friend Jenni over lunch to discuss the writing of this book. Jenni is one of the most brilliant women I know and she is a cherished friend and prayer warrior. I asked her to meet with me to talk over the subject of honoring your father and mother. Early in our conversation, I remember her saying, "This topic is huge!" I immediately agreed and said, "How in the world can I do it justice? I'm not a biblical scholar. I don't know Hebrew or Greek—others have spent their entire lives studying Scripture and I'm supposed to have something definitive to say on the subject?"

I'll never forget what Jenni said next: "Jan, you're right. There are others who know a great deal more than you do about what the Bible has to say when it comes to honoring our parents. But Jan, you have walked it. No one can tell your story but you."

I realized then what a tremendous undertaking this was. Most of us who've grown up in church have heard no less than a dozen sermons on the commandments. I remember as a child hearing that the fifth commandment was the only commandment with a promise. I was told that honoring your parents would result in "living a long life upon the earth." Even as a young child, I knew I didn't want to die anytime soon, so I knew I'd better figure out what it meant to honor my parents.

Although I've learned since that honoring your parents is not a guarantee of long life, it is a *commandment for life*. It is a commandment that we are to observe for our entire lifetime and it is a commandment that promises to provide a foundational stability for our life when followed.

Chapter 7

HONOR: WHAT THE BIBLE TEACHES

I realized early on that I needed help to understand more clearly the context and meaning of the fifth commandment. So I contacted two seminary professors seeking guidance. The first, Dr. John H. Sailhamer, whose PhD is in Ancient Near East Languages, is a professor at Golden Gate Seminary. My second interview was with Donald R. Sunukjian, ThD, PhD, professor of Preaching, and Department Chair of Christian Ministry Leadership at Talbot School of Theology at Biola University. In the course of my conversations with these two experts, I gleaned two surprising but fundamental aspects of the Bible's teachings about honor: First, honoring our parents involves *making them honorable* by treating them as such. Second, the command to honor our parents is a *command for life*—the requirement does not end with childhood, or even with the death of the parent. In what follows, I explore more fully the significance of these two insights.

Making Your Parents Honorable

My discussion with Dr. Sailhamer started with a quick look at the Hebrew word for honor used in the fifth commandment: *kabed*. Dr. Sailhamer said that *kabed* is "associated with glory, heaviness, worthiness, or importance."[1] He emphasized that the Hebrew and English languages are so different that it can be very difficult to capture the essence of the Hebrew meaning in the English language.

However, when I asked Dr. Sailhamer what "honor your father and mother" would have meant to the people of Israel at the time Moses gave them the Law, he answered, "to treat them as valuable." The original word has a "causative stem" which means it looks to the results: "as you treat them as valuable, they become valuable in your eyes."

"We are to honor them *as long as we live,* not only as long as *they live,*" he clarified. "It doesn't mean to treat them as honorable in the sense that we give them what they don't deserve. They deserve to be treated as honorable because they are."

As I sat with Dr. Sailhamer I couldn't help but think about the countless people I'd counseled over the years whose parents had not acted in honorable ways. The number one question that came up in the online survey that I conducted with men and women of all ages was this: "How do I honor my parents when they have acted in dishonorable ways?" When I posed this question to Dr. Sailhamer, he simply said that no matter how parents have acted we are to give them honor. But then he added this: in Hebrew the word implies "to make honorable. As godly children we're to do everything possible to make them honorable people. The worse off they are, the more they need godly children to help them live honorably."

I have to be honest. When he said those words, I asked myself, *and how in the world do you do that?* I could feel my stomach churning. I thought about a thirty-two-year-old woman I'd counseled who'd been sexually abused by her father from the time that she was six years old.

She'd aborted her father's baby at fifteen. At the time of our counseling sessions she was facing her third failed marriage and struggling in her relationship with God. I could imagine her justifiably angry protest at this idea: "After everything I've been through, you're telling me it is *my* responsibility to "make *him* honorable?"

As we talked further, Dr. Sailhamer emphasized, "Honor and obedience are tied together." He explained that when God gave the Law to Moses, the idea was that His people were to live accordingly and that each generation was accountable to pass on to the next generation the precepts of God. Honoring your parents meant you were to obey the godly commands taught by your parents as handed down by God.

I had to ask him again, this time with a different twist. "How do you honor parents who've not lived or taught you to live according to God's ways?"

He explained that we are to honor our parents *as if* they have taught us to walk in the ways of God. If parents have not lived honorably or taught us how to live a life that pleases God, we may demonstrate honor through *becoming* a parent who honors and obeys God. In effect, we "start a new chain, which is centered on teaching our children what God teaches us." Even when our parents have not acted honorably, we have a choice to live in ways that please God and thus we honor our parents through living rightly before God.

Dr. Sailhamer was explicit in saying that honoring our parents does not mean "blind obedience." Honoring your father and mother includes doing what is right. That means we are not bound by honor to disobey what God has clearly stated in His Word. When teaching his seminary students about honor Dr. Sailhamer admonishes, "Don't be judgmental, give respect to your parents, and keep trying to make them honorable."

This concept of "making them honorable" was perplexing. I walked away from our interview questioning what that would look like and if it was plausible. At the time, it was difficult for me to embrace, especially as I read some of the backgrounds and questions of those who responded to my survey. One male respondent wrote: "The biggest concern [I have about] 'honoring my parents' is when they are sinning. I've seen so many examples of personal friends whose fathers have cheated on their mothers, divorce situations, *major* criminal sins, and yet, you are to honor [them]?" *Lord*, I prayed, *there must be* some *exception*! What about a father or mother who was abusive? What about a mother who verbally assaulted you? What about parents who don't *deserve* the honor? Many respondents had suffered severe abuse, abandonment, or injury at the hands of one or both of their parents—but even so, they were expressing a desire to know how to honor parents under those conditions.

I thought about a woman I'd counseled years ago at a retreat whose parents were missionaries in Africa. She recounted how she'd been sexually abused by a trusted friend of her parents, a tribal leader who'd offered to teach her how to play a musical instrument as his means to gain access to her. The abuse continued for several years until she finally told her parents about it when they came back to the States on furlough. Her parents were emphatic: she must have misunderstood his actions. They told her to keep quiet, forgive the tribal leader, and forget what happened because otherwise their ministry in Africa would be jeopardized. I'll never forget her questions: "How do I honor parents who abandoned me for the sake of their image and ministry?"

There are no easy answers to such questions. And those who try to answer them run the risk of minimizing the injury and pain of the one who has suffered. Some go so far as to suggest that the spiritual benefits to the kingdom somehow outweighed the physical or emotional wrongs suffered.

Honor for Life

I took up these difficult questions in my interview with Dr. Sunukjian. "Are all parents *worthy* of honor?" I asked. Dr. Sunukjian paused and then thoughtfully said, "All parents are to *be* honored. The assumption is they've done something to deserve it. Whether it was giving us birth, keeping us alive, taking care of us, feeding us, clothing us, or housing us, the idea is that they contributed to sustaining our life. Had they not done so, we would have died."[2] He added that while we have a "huge indebtedness to them, there's obviously a great spectrum of failure from terrible abuse to minor foolishness." Even when parents have failed, there is a "legitimate debt" that we owe them, which is expressed through our honor.

Dr. Sunukjian clarified that we are "indebted to every parent who did the parenting job on us." In other words, "it's the one who raised us" that we're to honor. "So," I interjected, "since my parents divorced when I was five and my mother remarried when I was eight, my biblical responsibility to honor my parents applies to my mother and stepfather who raised me?"

"Yes," Dr. Sunukjian said. "You may choose to honor your biological parent, but biblically speaking your requirement is to give honor to those who parented you from childhood through to adulthood."

I asked Dr. Sunukjian, who has five adult children of his own, what it means to honor our parents. He responded, "I attach a special significance to them. I attach substance to them. In Hebrew it literally means to 'give weight to your parents in your life.' Simply put, it means 'they are important in your eyes.'"

When reading Exodus 20 and Deuteronomy 5, I'd always wondered why the command to honor your parents was the only command with a promise attached. It seemed to say that those who honor their parents will have a long life: "Honor your father and your mother, so that you may live long in the land the LORD your God is giving you" (Exodus 20:12 NIV).

I asked Dr. Sunukjian why he thought this was the only command given with a promise. He sat pensively and then replied, "One possible answer is that when we honor our parents, the natural outworking of that action has a physiological benefit. In Exodus when the command was originally given, it meant that the nation of Israel would have a long duration of life in the land of promise. The apostle Paul makes it individualized in the New Testament when he says 'you will live long on the earth.' It seems to indicate that the natural outcome of honoring your parents is that it tends to produce longevity of life."

This was a profound idea. This is not to say that we should apply this principle conversely. In other words, if a person dies at a young age we should not assume they failed to follow the command to honor. Nor does it imply that all those who live long were stellar in their efforts to honor their parents. What it may suggest is that, generally speaking, when we honor our parents we are endowed with stability and peacefulness, resulting in longevity.

Dr. Sunukjian believes that Scripture points to three distinct stages of honoring our parents. He suggests that as children, the way that we honor is through obedience according to Ephesians 6:1. The next stage is that of adulthood; in this stage of life, honor means that we "regard, respect, and show reverence toward our parents." He said it is an attitude of the heart that means "we show deference toward our parents by esteeming them and respecting their position." Finally, honoring our parents is demonstrated in our parents' latter years by making financial provision for them as needed. We make a commitment to "love them to the end" of their life and we are ready to lend financial support as a means of expressing our honor. He summarized by saying that honoring our parents goes from "obedience, to respect and revering, and finally to financial provision for our aging parents."

As I listened, all kinds of questions and objections came to my mind: What if your parents were alcoholics who squandered all their resources as a result of their drinking? As an adult child, are you to bear the burden of their care even though they lived irresponsibly? Does this mean I have to provide financial support to an ungodly lifestyle? Am I to fund their extravagances or only their needs? What if providing for them puts undue strain upon my own family's financial needs? I checked myself before firing off these questions. I realized the questions themselves were indicative of my own heart attitude! I was making a case in my mind for all the exceptions, rather than seeking a practical understanding of what this might look like for others and myself.

This practice of caring for aging parents is a given in some cultures. But here in the States, it's not uncommon to find a nursing home or assisted living facility for our aging parents rather than take them into our home. In many cultures, this would be a shameful practice. Jesus Himself condemned the Pharisees in Matthew 15:3–7 for following a tradition that exempted them from providing financial care for parents. He indicted them for adopting this exemption because in so doing, they failed to keep the Law of Moses that required honoring one's parents through financial provision.

In talking about these different stages of honor, I had to ask Dr. Sunukjian about the transition from childhood to adulthood. I was thinking about the many single adults and young couples I've counseled who struggle with knowing how to transition from the "obedience stage" to the "respecting and revering stage." Many have shared with me that they are ready to make that transition, but their parents are not.

I thought of Stacy, a young newlywed, who sat in my office in tears, distraught over her strained relationship with her parents. She described how, prior to the wedding, her parents seemed to love her husband-to-be, Scott, and that they all enjoyed time together during their engagement. But later, when Scott's job required a move from the east coast to the west coast, her parents were overcome with disappointment. They told her that Scott must not love her that much if he was willing to uproot her from her family and close friends. Even though she and Scott had only been married six months, her parents were already talking about how awful it would be for her as a young mother of children not to have her family around to help support her in the early years of motherhood. Her mother became so resentful toward her husband Scott that she refused to talk with him. She began pressuring Stacy to tell Scott that she should refuse to move and suggest that Scott go to work for her father. Scott had no intention of working for her father and told Stacy that this move was a step for their future. When Stacy tried to reason with her parents they were adamant. Stacy was disregarding their wisdom, and was therefore "dishonoring" them.

"I love my husband, but I also love and respect my parents. How am I to 'leave and cleave' and 'honor my parents' at the same time?" Stacy asked in desperation.

I posed a similar question to Dr. Sunukjian. He said, "Parents have to release the adult child from obedience and the adult child must learn to maintain respect and reverence." In the above scenario, it might look like this: Stacy sits down with her parents and says, "Mom and Dad, I know that you want me to stay in this area and not make the move. I want you to know that I love you and am grateful for all that you've done for me. But Scott and I have given this decision a lot of thought, prayer, and consideration, and we've decided that we are going to make the move. We know that you're going to be disappointed, but we hope you can respect our decision. We'll do all that we can to stay connected through email and phone calls and we hope you'll consider visiting us once we get settled."

Dr. Sunukjian said, "Revering and honoring doesn't mean that I always do what my parents wish I would do." He clarified that it primarily means that when I'm in their presence I am polite, respectful, and conciliatory as opposed to picking a fight, criticizing, finding fault, or quick to take up an argument. It means that I find a way to keep our relationship peaceful.

Dr. Sunukjian pointed out a clear distinction: Each person is responsible before God to follow the command to "honor your father and mother," but a parent is not the one to decide whether or not their adult child's behavior is "honoring or dishonoring." Parents are certainly entitled to an opinion; however, the adult child stands before God and is accountable to Him alone for their actions. Dr. Sunukjian continued, "Honoring is how I treat my parents, not whether I do what they want. If my grown son believes in his heart he is honoring me, it's not for me to say he's not." Our attitude toward our parents should always be characterized by the "gentleness of Christ" and should say to them and others, "you are important in my life."

Old Testament Law or New Testament Grace?

Some of you might be thinking, *that's all well and good, but the command was given in the Old Testament and now in Christ we are not under the bondage of the Law.* It's true that we live under the new covenant as outlined for us in the New Testament. But the fact is that the New Testament doesn't simply abolish the Old. In fact, the New Testament often fulfills the Old Testament in a way that confirms or even extends aspects of the Old Testament. The fifth commandment is no exception.

What does the New Testament say with regard to honoring our parents? The Greek word for honor is the word *timao* and it means "to prize; fix a valuation upon; to revere; to honor." It conveys the same idea as in the Old Testament, that one show respect and give recognition to those to whom it is directed.[3] As a matter of fact, in three of four gospel records, Jesus quotes the Old Testament command to "honor your father and mother"[4] (Matthew 15:4; 19:19; Mark 7:10; 10:19; Luke 18:20). Two gospels record Jesus' indictment of the Pharisees who were following a tradition whereby they could exempt themselves from helping their parents financially by claiming that certain money had been devoted to God, as was mentioned earlier.[5]

There are three other New Testament passages worth mentioning here. The first is well known, as it is the apostle Paul's directive to children: "Children, obey your parents in the Lord, for this is right. 'Honor your father and mother'—which is the first commandment with a promise—'so that it may go well with you and that you may enjoy long life on the earth'" (Ephesians 6:1–3 NIV).

As explained earlier by Dr. Sunukjian, this passage seems to deal with the first two stages of honor: the stage of childhood obedience, and the stage of respect and reverence appropriate for adult children, resulting in stability and longevity of life. Paul writes a similar directive to children in Colossians 3:20, indicating that obedience to parents "pleases the Lord" (NIV). The final passage is less familiar, but important to cite. It appears in Paul's letter to Timothy, his "son" in the faith, and it conveys what Dr. Sunukjian described earlier as the "legitimate debt" owed to our parents and grandparents as well. "But if a widow has children or grandchildren, these should learn first of all to put their religion into practice by caring for their own family and so repaying their parents and grandparents, for this is pleasing to God" (1 Timothy 5:4 NIV).

It's clear from Jesus' teaching and Paul's instructions to the church that honoring our parents is a vital part of living a life that is honoring to God. It's also clear from other passages that as New Testament believers, we are not "under" the law. But the law, as expressed in the Ten Commandments, remains as a guide for us to live by and is declared by Paul to be "holy righteous and good" (Romans 7:12 NIV).

Time-Honored Truth

Several years ago I audited a seminary class on expository preaching taught by Dr. Sunukjian. The class was full of young seminarians who had a deep desire to exposit the Scripture accurately and eloquently. In the process of learning how to prepare a sermon, we learned about the importance of context and how to draw out the central theme of any given passage as intended by the author.

Dr. Sunukjian explained to the aspiring pastors that their job was to communicate God's "time-honored truth" effectively to their congregations by making the passage relevant to their audience. I remember sitting in the class thinking, *how can I expect to grasp God's time-honored truth in a passage, let alone make it relevant and communicate it effectively to others?*

I'm feeling that same sense right now. It is a daunting task to try to flesh out all that we have learned about honor in this chapter. What I know to be true is that God placed the fifth commandment—"to honor your father and mother"—in the very center of the list of the Ten Commandments. The Ten Commandments were given as practical guidelines for God's people to live a life that is healthy, holy, and God-honoring.

It is said that the first four commandments deal with our covenantal relationship with God and the last six give emphasis to our relationship with others. It seems to follow that placing the command to honor our parents in the very center between our unrivaled devotion to God and our commitment to love others is profound. It says to me that inherent in this command to honor our parents is a foundational, life-altering principle that when followed promises to secure stability of life and pass on a legacy for our children and future generations. I'm not sure that I understand all of the vast implications of God's intentions when he gave us this command, but I do want to invite you, dear reader, to consider how adherence to this command might look in your life. I have been challenged to do the same. The rest of this book is dedicated to the purpose of giving you a glimpse of walking out this command in practical ways.

For now, let me see if I can summarize what I learned through these interviews as it relates to my life and story. At first, the principle of *making parents honorable* as described by Dr. Sailhamer was a bit hard to swallow. I pondered it for several days and prayed that I might see from God's perspective what this might look like in my life.

I was humbled when God answered. He reminded me that after several months of gut-wrenching counseling in my late twenties, I was able to consider confronting my parents with the abuse. My desire was to reconcile the relationship through forgiveness and the setting of some appropriate boundaries. It took me a couple years of grieving through the losses associated with the abuse to come to this place. Eventually, my stepfather confessed to what he had done and I lovingly told him that by God's grace I had forgiven him.

I expressed my desire to rebuild our relationship with two important stipulations: first, that we would speak truthfully and directly with each other from this point on; and second, that my children would never stay in their home. Even though my stepfather said he would never abuse my children, neither he nor my mother had taken steps toward their own healing, something that might have allowed me to trust them to care appropriately for my children. The Lord seemed to impress upon me that when I made that decision and implemented that specific boundary, I had in effect, "made my parents honorable." Through implementing the boundary, I did not allow them the opportunity to replicate the sinful patterns that had played out in my life; with God's help, a new pattern was being established. I didn't realize it then, but God was teaching me about what it means to honor. I was respectful both in my heart and my communication with them while at the same time holding firmly to what I knew was an important safeguard.

It may become clearer as you continue reading what form "making your parents honorable" may take in your life and relationship. For now, I'd invite you simply to ask God to open your heart to His direction and to allow His Spirit to teach you what it looks like in your life to honor your father and mother.

When reflecting on what I learned from Dr. Sunukjian, I was moved by his strong admonition that the fifth commandment is a *commandment for life*: we are called to honor our parents throughout our lifetime, in three distinct stages. As children we honor our parents through our obedience; as adults we honor them through respectful attitudes, actions, conciliatory communication; and finally, we show honor through financial provision for our aging parents.

Keeping this commandment takes various forms depending on our specific situations. One of the ways I honor my parents is to make changes in my life and family that are more representative of God's guidelines for living as shown to us in Scripture. I honor my parents for any godly values I was taught by continuing to model those values to my children and eventually to my grandchildren.

But I also honor my parents by *changing* certain patterns that were sinful, destructive, or dysfunctional in nature. How can this be honoring to your parents when you are *changing* something from your upbringing? Remember that honoring our parents doesn't mean enshrining them as saints or refusing to acknowledge their shortcomings. It means we accept them as fallen, broken people and *learn* from what they taught us. We "give weight" to all that we received from them and respond to it through the full counsel of God, making changes by God's grace where necessary. This learning, growing, and maturing process in itself brings honor to our parents because we're living a life that is honoring to God and we're passing on new patterns to future generations.

Think of it this way. As we look in Scripture to the "fathers of our faith,"—Abraham, Sarah, Moses, Gideon, Samuel, David, Rahab and Peter—we see them as real people with strengths and weaknesses. We see they made choices that reflected great faith in God as well as choices that evidenced their lack of faith. In 1 Corinthians 10:6, 11a, Paul exhorts us to learn from the example of those who have gone before us, particularly the Israelites' history in the wilderness: "Now these things occurred as examples to keep us from setting our hearts on evil things as they did. . . . These things happened to them as examples and were written down as warnings for us" (NIV). The life stories of the "fathers of our faith" are recorded in Scripture for our benefit that we might *learn* from their example.

So it is with our parents. When we choose to learn from our experiences and implement godly change we honor our parents. It is a lifetime process and a commitment to honor that will sustain us through each generation as we take to heart this fifth commandment to "honor our father and mother."

Chapter 8

HONOR: WHAT JESUS' LIFE TEACHES

Have you ever wondered what it might have looked like to grow up in Jesus' family of nine?[1] How would you handle having a perfect child in the midst of all the usual conflicts and petty arguments that happen in most families? Think about Jesus, his siblings, Mary, and Joseph eating dinner around the table, going to synagogue, working, and playing—what do you envision about their interactions?

We have a limited picture of those interactions in Scripture. There are four snapshots of Jesus and his family and only one of them involves Joseph, Jesus' earthly father; the rest are with Mary, his mother.[2] I was familiar with each of the passages, but I had never read them together and I had never taken time to consider them thoughtfully. What, if anything, can we learn or understand from Jesus' relationship with his parents? Is he in a special category because of his divine nature when it comes to his earthly relationship with His parents or are there principles that are relevant for us today? How do we experience these interactions as we read them and what are they telling us about God, ourselves, and our relationship with our parents?

Jesus Stays Behind

The first passage we want to examine is Luke 2:41–52. In this passage, Joseph, Mary, and Jesus go to Jerusalem for the yearly Passover Feast. Jesus was twelve years old at the time, which in Jewish culture was the year before he would ceremonially celebrate his passage into manhood at age thirteen.

It was customary for families to travel from their hometowns to Jerusalem in large caravans. The trip from Nazareth to Jerusalem normally took three days.[3] After celebrating the feast they headed for home and at the end of the first day Mary and Joseph began looking for Jesus among their relatives, but could not find him. They were unaware that he had stayed behind in Jerusalem. It was probably a classic case familiar to many parents: "I thought he was with you!" Mary said with concern to Joseph. "No, I haven't seen him since we left." "Oh, dear! He's not with our relatives either—where do you think he is? Oh Yahweh, please don't let any harm come to him before we can get to him!"

After realizing Jesus is not in the caravan, Mary and Joseph turn around and make the day's journey back to Jerusalem. Once they arrive in Jerusalem, they look for Jesus for an entire day, but they don't find him. By the time they find him he has been missing for three days—one day out with the caravan, another day back, and one day looking for him.[4]

If you're a parent reading this, you know this is panic time. You mentally run through various scenarios of what might have happened to your child, not wanting to say them out loud because they are too frightening to verbalize. You are beating yourself up (or finding ways to blame your mate) for the lack of parental responsibility. You can't imagine what your

Honoring Dishonorable Parents

twelve year old has done for food, shelter, and safety over the last seventy-two hours!

Mary and Joseph make their way back to the temple where they find Jesus, "sitting among the teachers, listening to them, and asking questions." The text tells us that everyone in the temple was "amazed at his understanding and his answers."

When I thought about this scene, I imagined it might be like heading home after a visit to one of the museums at the Smithsonian Institute in Washington, D.C. only to realize your child is missing. Upon returning to the city, you find him at the museum conducting a seminar for the curator, historical experts, tour guides, and tourists on the authenticity of the Dead Sea Scrolls!

I love Mary's initial response because it is so typical of mothers, "Son, why have you treated us like this? Your father and I have been anxiously searching for you." The word *anxiously* in the Greek means "to cause pain, consuming grief or distress."[5] In modern day terms we might say Mary was "heartsick" over Jesus' unknown whereabouts and she let him know it!

Now look carefully at Jesus' response. Keep in mind, he is twelve years old and has been unaccounted for in Jerusalem for four days. "Why were you searching for me?" he asked. "Didn't you know I had to be in my Father's house?"

What is your reaction as you read Jesus' words? To be honest, my first reaction was "Whoa, Jesus sounds a little disrespectful." He seems to have a tone of chastisement toward Mary and Joseph for their lack of attunement to his mission. But upon further consideration I had to chuckle a bit. Jesus was perfectly within the bounds of His divine nature and His humanity. He was exercising what all parents of adolescents experience—the transition of their children into adults.

Commentators note that this is the first mention of Jesus' awareness of His divine parentage and that Jesus was delineating between His relationship with His earthly parents and His true Father. Later in His ministry, Jesus would call His own followers to the same devotion to God that He models. In Matthew 10: 34–37, He unequivocally tells his disciples:

> Do not suppose that I have come to bring peace to the earth. I did not come to bring peace, but a sword. For I have come to turn 'a man against his father, a daughter against her mother, a daughter-in-law against her mother-in-law—a man's enemies will be the members of his own household.' Anyone who loves their father or mother more than me is not worthy of me; anyone who loves their son or daughter more than me is not worthy of me. (NIV)

This incident between Jesus and His earthly parents also seems to be the first "installment" of Simeon's prophecy given to Mary in Luke 2 when he tells her that "a sword will pierce her soul." As a mother, she would have to learn to let go and relinquish Jesus to the Father's will throughout His life, and ultimately to His death on a cross. Jesus made sure that His parents knew that He was clear about His mission and whose authority would take precedence in His life. But the text indicates that Mary and Joseph didn't understand—they weren't fully tracking with what Jesus was saying to them.

The story does not end there. We are given a broad stroke of the next eighteen years of Jesus' life: "Then he went down to Nazareth with them and was obedient to them. But his mother treasured all these things in her heart. And Jesus grew in wisdom and stature, and in favor with God and man" (Luke 2:51–52 NIV).

The thought conveyed in these verses is that Jesus willingly submitted to the authority of His parents while remaining in their home and until His entry into His public ministry. The Greek word used here for "obedient" is *hypotasso*, which originally was a military term meaning to be "arranged or ordered under the command of a leader."[6] In effect, Jesus voluntarily subjected Himself to the God-given authority of His parents until the time set by the Father for His public ministry to begin. Commentators believe that it was during those years that Joseph died, leaving Mary a widow and Jesus as the firstborn son financially responsible for the family.[7]

Does this passage surprise you in any way? What do you notice about Jesus? What can we learn about honoring our mother and father from this passage? When I was talking to a friend about writing this book she mentioned this passage, remarking that it is the only passage in Scripture that speaks of Jesus' early life with his parents. When I sat down to read it with this fact in mind, I was somewhat perplexed. Why would God inspire Luke to depict *this* snapshot alone from Jesus' childhood? Why didn't Luke record Jesus demonstrating some generous act of kindness toward His mother? Or why wasn't Jesus shown in Joseph's carpentry shop learning His earthly father's trade? Surely there must have been times when Jesus saw His parents and one of His brothers or sisters exchange harsh words with each other. Wouldn't it have seemed fitting to record Him offering words of wisdom and "calming the emotional storm" that was permeating their home?

Instead, we read this account of Jesus purposely staying behind in Jerusalem without His parent's knowledge or consent. We see Him in no hurry to leave the city; and in fact, He is engaged in dialogue with the religious leaders when His parents finally find Him. When asked why He has been rather insensitive to His parents' concern, Jesus replies that His parents should have known His higher responsibility was to God, His true Father. Then, in striking contrast, we're told that Jesus willingly returns with His parents to Nazareth where He spends the next eighteen years being subject to their authority. It is there that He grows in maturity and finds "favor with God and men."

The Ideal Wedding Guest

Our second passage is only in John's gospel and is probably the most well known. I suppose there are three reasons for its popularity. First, it is the first recorded miracle Jesus performed; second, it takes place at a wedding celebration; and third, it involved turning water into wine!

The text tells us that there is a wedding in Cana of Galilee and Jesus' mother Mary was there and that Jesus and his disciples were also invited to the wedding. In that culture wedding feasts often lasted seven days.[8] Sometime during the latter part of the celebration, when Mary informs Jesus that "they have no more wine," Jesus replies, "Dear woman, why do you involve me? My time has not yet come."

At first glance most readers would be surprised by Jesus' addressing his mother as "Dear woman," but commentators say this was a polite, kind expression of that day.[9] However, Jesus' question that followed has a different tone. In current vernacular, the question would be, "What is it to me and you that they're out of wine?" Then he adds, "My time has not yet come."

Essentially, Jesus was saying to Mary that he was committed to God the Father's will—which included the exact time that He was to make Himself known. As one author put it, "As Jesus began his public life, his first miracle gave him the occasion for impressing his mother with the fact that she must no longer impose her will and wishes upon him."[10]

I find it interesting that after Jesus' mild rebuff, Mary gives the servants instructions to "do whatever he tells you." There must have been something inside her that knew her son would respond, even though she didn't know how. Jesus instructs the servants to fill six jars with water, each holding between twenty to thirty gallons, and then to take a sample of the contents to the master of the banquet. The master of the banquet tasted the water that Jesus turned into wine and called the bridegroom aside to extol him for "saving the best wine for last."

This miracle was distinctive for two reasons. First, it was of a private nature and was only known by the disciples, Mary, and the servants who filled the water jars. Second, it didn't involve relieving human misery but was a generous act of kindness that alleviated possible embarrassment for the bridegroom and his family.

I couldn't help but relate a little. When our oldest daughter Heather married our son-in-law Eric, the ceremony and dinner reception took place at a winery in California. It was a beautiful sunset wedding and the evening sky "declared the glory of God." As dinner was served, my husband took his first bite to discover his food was lukewarm. I promptly took a bite from my plate to confirm his findings. I proceeded to take a survey at surrounding tables only to find out that most of our guests' entrées were warm at best. Many guests were reluctant to be truthful, wanting to spare us embarrassment, but the fact remained that the only guests whose food was served hot were those who had ordered fish. I immediately discussed the issue with the wedding coordinator, but with most guests already served, there was no remedy available. All of our guests were wonderfully gracious and commented on the beauty of the wedding and the festive celebration that followed, but as parents of the bride and hosts of the wedding we were a little embarrassed. As I thought about our experience, I entertained the idea that had Jesus and His mother been present, the outcome might have been different!

John gives us insight into God's purpose for the miracle in verse 11. "He [Jesus] thus revealed his glory, and his disciples put their faith in him." Interestingly, it does not say anything of Mary's thoughts or feelings, but I'm sure as in times past, she "pondered all these things in her heart."

It is thought by some that Jesus left Nazareth just prior to this event, never to return home.[11] It seems clear that with the entrance into His public ministry, Jesus subordinates Mary's influence to the will of God.

Jesus Ruffles Family Feathers

The next passage I want to examine is Mark 3:31–34. This familial interaction is also recorded in Matthew 12:46–50, and again in Luke 8:19–21. Mark seems to give us greater detail so it is helpful to look at the beginning of the chapter to gain the larger context of the passage.

At the beginning of chapter 3, Jesus is at the synagogue, probably in Capernaum, with a man whose hand is shriveled. The Pharisees were watching Him closely to see if He would "break the Sabbath law" by healing the man. They only permitted healing on the Sabbath if a person's life was in danger.[12] Jesus, knowing their thoughts, asks them a rhetorical question: "Which is lawful on the Sabbath: to do good or to do evil, to save life or to kill?" (Mark 3:4 NIV). Everyone remained silent. The text tells us that Jesus looked around at them in anger and that He was "deeply distressed at their stubborn hearts." This is the only explicit reference to Jesus' anger in the New Testament and it was "coupled with a deep grief at the Pharisees' obstinate insensitivity to God's mercy and human misery."[13] He then commanded the man to stretch out his hand. With every eye riveted on him, the man reaches forth his hand and it is completely restored; the bones are strong again, his fingers are rightly shaped, the blood is flowing through the veins of his hand, and he can make a fist and shake another's hand for the first time in years.

There's an immediate reaction by those watching. Not of gratitude, nor of wonder. The Pharisees together with the Herodians begin to plot together about how they "might kill Jesus" (Mark 3:6 NIV).

We see from verses 7 through 13 that Jesus' ministry to the sick and demon-possessed has expanded, causing huge crowds to form around him. Jesus tells His disciples to get a small boat ready for a quick getaway because the crowds were pressing in on Him.[14] He retreats with His disciples for a period of time before engaging once again with the crowd.

Then we're told something in verses 20 through 21 that neither of the other gospel writers record: "Jesus entered a house, and again a crowd gathered, so that he and his disciples were not even able to eat. When his family heard about this, they went to take charge of him, for they said, 'He is out of his mind.'"

Jesus' mother and brothers apparently traveled from Nazareth in order to "take charge of him." This word in the Greek means "to take hold of, grasp, meaning to have power over, rule over."[15] It's a strong word that implies that Jesus' mother and brothers wanted to take Him away, even if by force. What was this about? Had they heard the reports in Nazareth that Jesus was upsetting the religious community by healing on the Sabbath? Was the family experiencing criticism due to Jesus' increasingly controversial ministry?

The text seems to indicate that they were concerned for Jesus' well-being due to His ceaseless activity and they thought He was out of His mind due to the claims He was making.[16] I have to wonder if maybe it was Mary whose protective instincts garnered the cooperation of her other sons. She may have heard about Jesus' popularity and the schedule He was keeping and decided to rally her other sons and run to the rescue. I'm not so sure that Jesus' brothers were motivated by their mother's concerns as much as their need to preserve the family's reputation. After all, the rulers of the synagogue carried a lot of weight in and around Jerusalem. His brothers knew the people in Jesus' hometown of Nazareth disbelieved Him and were ready to throw Him over a cliff on one occasion for His indictment of their unbelief (Luke 4:28–30). John tells us that Jesus' brothers did not believe in him until after the resurrection (John 7:5; Acts 1:4). Regardless of Mary and Jesus' brothers' motivations, it's clear from the text that they were on a mission to restrain his ministry.

When Mary and Jesus' brothers arrived at the scene, they sent a messenger into the house to tell Jesus they are outside. Listen to Jesus' response: "'Who are my mother and my brothers?' he asked. Then he looked at those seated in a circle around him and said, 'Here are my mother and my brothers! Whoever does God's will is my brother and sister and mother'" (Mark 3:33–35 NIV). In Matthew's account of the event, Jesus points to his disciples and says, "Here are my mother and my brothers. For whoever does the will of my Father in heaven is my brother and sister and mother" (Matthew 12:49–50 NIV).

Commentators agree that Jesus was not being dismissive of his family relationships—he was emphasizing a higher priority. He was telling those around Him that doing the will of God, His true Father, created a spiritual kinship that was far greater than any biological ties.[17] The parallel passage in Luke 8:21 makes it clearer: "My mother and brothers are those who hear God's word and put it into practice" (NIV).

There's no doubt that Jesus had to repeat these words to His mother and brothers. He had to make clear to them that His obedience to the Father took precedence. In effect, He had to delineate the boundary lines between family and God when it came to obedience. It was another occasion for Mary to learn to submit to the One to Whom she had given birth.

Jesus Makes Provisions from the Cross

The final snapshot appears in John 19:25–27. This is the most tender of all the passages we've looked at thus far. "Near the cross of Jesus stood his mother, his mother's sister, Mary the wife of Clopas, and Mary Magdalene. When Jesus saw his mother there, and the disciple whom he loved standing nearby, he said to her, 'Woman, here is your son,' and to the disciple, 'Here is your mother.' From that time on, this disciple took her into his home" (NIV).[18]

Now, take a journey back in time to better understand the scene of Jesus' last recorded interaction with His mother, Mary. Imagine yourself walking the road to Golgotha as one of Jesus' followers. You've heard His teachings, seen Him miraculously heal the sick. You've witnessed the raising of Lazarus from the dead, and you've seen demon-possessed people delivered from torment and regain their sanity.

You believe Jesus is the long awaited, promised Messiah who would bring redemption to the people of Israel. But now, as you watch Jesus fall under the weight of the crossbeam on His way to Golgotha, he doesn't look like the Messiah. He is barely recognizable. He has been beaten and His face is bloodied and swollen. You see the crown of thorns on His brow and the flesh on His back ripped open from being flogged.

You arrive at the place called Golgotha and hear the soldiers mocking Him. The chief priests are sneering and ridiculing Him while many others are hurling insults at Him, including one of the criminals sentenced to die alongside Him. The grief-stricken wails of some of the women are so loud you can barely hear yourself think. Just after you arrive, the soldiers strip Jesus naked, lay him on the ground with both arms outstretched, and nail His forearms to the crossbeam. Blood gushes from His limbs as Jesus' executioners raise the beam and fasten it to the upright post embedded in the ground. Finally, they nail Jesus' feet to the cross.[19] The soldiers throw dice to see who will get His personal belongings, not knowing that their actions fulfill an Old Testament prophecy (Psalm 22:18).

And then, you see her. Mary, the mother of Jesus, is standing near the foot of the cross. She has witnessed it all. She is there with three other women and a man, all of whom you recognize as being followers of Jesus. You catch no glimpse of the other disciples who had walked with Jesus healing the sick, restoring sight to the blind, and speaking gracious words of life and hope. You wonder where they are. You're not aware that all of them scattered when Jesus was taken into custody. You learn later that one of Jesus' disciples, Judas, had betrayed Him, while another, Peter, had denied three times that he even knew Jesus, just to save his own skin.

But here at the foot of the cross stands Mary. You can't begin to grasp the anguish she must feel. It is difficult enough for you to see him hanging there . . . bloodied, beaten, broken. You edge your way a little closer through the angry crowd shouting for Him to "save himself"—taunting Him with their words. Just as you are about to turn away, you see Him looking at His mother through eyes nearly swollen shut and hear His barely audible voice say, "Dear woman, here is your son," and to the disciple standing nearby, "Here is your mother." Tears fill your eyes as you realize you are witnessing Jesus' parting words to His mother.

John's Gospel is the only one that records Christ's final words to Mary. We know from the text that the disciple who took Mary into his home from that time on was John himself, the disciple whom Jesus loved, one of the twelve, and a cousin to Jesus.[20]

Commentators can only speculate as to why Jesus called upon John, rather than His other brothers or sisters, to carry out the duties of the eldest brother in caring for His mother. Some speculate that in John's home Mary would find the spiritual atmosphere that would suit her thirst for God and she would find in John a "son" whom she would grow to love as well.[21] Another possibility could have been that Jesus' siblings were in Galilee and not in a position to care for her.[22]

I wonder if Jesus, given his intimate knowledge of both Mary and John, knew they would greatly benefit from each other due to their shared love for and commitment to Him. It would seem that choosing John to care for His mother was not just a financial provision, but an emotional provision as well. We don't know when or how Mary died, but perhaps Jesus chose the apostle John because of his life expectancy. He outlived the rest of the disciples, including Jesus' own half-brother James (the head of the Jerusalem church) who was martyred in AD 62.

In all the other passages we've examined, we have seen Mary as the one who is displaying some type of emotion: at the temple scene she admitted to being anxious when searching for the boy Jesus; at the wedding in Cana she displayed concern over a socially awkward situation which initiated her desire for Jesus' involvement; and in Capernaum she expressed her worry over Jesus' well-being. Here, at the foot of the cross, we are left to imagine Mary's thoughts. John records nothing of her emotional state—Jesus is the one in this scene who is showing deep compassion, even amidst His excruciating suffering. He looks tenderly upon His mother standing beneath the cross and makes provisions for the rest of her earthly pilgrimage. Scripture contains no other recorded interaction between them. The last reference to Mary is in Acts 1:14, after Jesus' ascension into heaven. She is among the disciples, Jesus' brothers, and other believers who are waiting and praying for the promised Holy Spirit, in obedience to Jesus' instructions (Acts 1:4–5). One commentator suggests that "In that moment the tremendous truth must at last have dawned upon Mary, that He who hung upon the cross was not her son; that before the world was He was; that so far from being His mother, she was herself His child."[23]

Go and Do Likewise

As you reflect on these four scenes, what observations have you made? What were your impressions of Jesus' interactions with His parents? Are there any principles that can be gleaned that are relevant for you today? Can we really expect to draw truths applicable to our own lives from these depictions of Jesus' unique relationship with His parents? Do these narratives speak to us concerning what it means to honor our parents in a culture such as ours, with fractured families, soaring divorce rates, and rampant child abuse?

One of my favorite verses in all of Scripture is Romans 15:4: "For *everything* that was written in the past was written to teach us, so that through the endurance taught in the Scriptures and the encouragement they provide we might have hope" (NIV, emphasis added). As I've sat with these passages depicting Jesus' interaction with His parents, I've asked myself what is characteristic about them. What, essentially, is being conveyed about Jesus' way of honoring His parents?

Two words come to mind: *respectful* and *responsive*. As I observe Jesus in relation to His earthly parents, He is *respectful* of their God-given position of authority over Him, and He *responds* to them willingly. He is *respectful* of the culture in which He lives while at the same time staying true to His calling. Finally, He remains *respectful* even when His family doesn't understand His mission and calling. He maintains connection with His mother and siblings throughout His life and ministry.

Jesus is *responsive* to His parents and family, choosing to communicate and clarify His mission. He *responds* to their concerns without compromising His calling. He is *responsive*, not reactive. He stays clear about His purpose while showing honor and sensitivity to His mother and her needs.

What strikes me most is that Jesus is able perfectly to hold the tension between honoring His earthly parents while faithfully carrying out His Father's will, even when the two responsibilities seem to be in conflict. For many of us, that is our struggle as well:

- How do I honor my parents and keep my spouse a priority?
- How do I respond when their desire for my life seems in conflict with what I believe to be God's direction at this time?
- How do I honor them in their old age, when what they want is so different from what they really need?

Jesus shows us that it is possible to honor our parents in the midst of misunderstanding, disagreement, and confusion. He models for us the willingness to remain humbly in subjection for a season without compromising obedience to God's call.

We've learned from the life of Jesus that honoring entails being respectful and responsive to our parents throughout our lifetime. It is a commandment for life. We can be assured that God will enable us to do what He's commanded us to do as we humbly seek to follow Jesus' example. We turn now to look more specifically at how honor is lived out in adulthood. If you struggle with honoring *dishonorable* parents, don't stop reading. You will be provided with some practical guidelines for honoring your parents no matter what your circumstances may be.

SECTION III

HONOR LIVED OUT IN ADULTHOOD

My dear friend and spiritual "mother," Dotty Stephenson, is eighty-six years old at the time of writing. She was my fifth grade Sunday school teacher. Her son John and I liked each other in elementary school. I lost track of Dotty after our family relocated to a neighboring city about thirty miles away when I was in junior high. Her son John and I stayed in contact for a while, but we lost contact after high school.

In my early thirties, I was invited to share my testimony at a church not far from the church I attended as a child. I shared about how I received Jesus into my heart at the age of ten. I shared briefly about the sexual abuse in my family and the process God brought me through to healing. After I finished speaking, a woman ran up to me from the audience and put her arms around me, embracing me tightly. Through tears she said, "Oh honey, I'm so sorry, I didn't know. I wish I had known. Oh honey, I'm so sorry that happened to you." I stepped back, and standing before me was Dotty. She hadn't recognized my name on the program since I was now married and had a different last name, but as she sat in the audience listening to my story, she quickly realized who I was. She had known my parents and was shocked by the events that had gripped our family. From that time on, we have stayed in close contact and she is one of my precious prayer warriors and spiritual mentors.

Dotty's son John struggled in his walk with God for many years in his early adulthood. Dotty was the first to admit that she had not been a perfect mother, but she continued to pray faithfully for John over the years. Often as we sat together over lunch and I would ask how John was doing, she would say, "He's having a time of it right now," but with faith-filled laughter she'd add, "I know God is at work and I'm just going to praise Him!" When my daughter Heather was going through adolescence I called Dotty on more than one occasion for counsel; it was always the same: "Just keep praying and praising, honey, she'll come around!"

Dotty prayed for John for over twenty three years and she rejoiced to see the day that he fully committed his heart and life to the lordship of Jesus Christ. I had the occasion to have lunch with Dotty and John a few years ago. It had been about thirty five years since I'd seen him and it was a joy to hear how God had faithfully worked in his life. He had gone through some rough times: a couple of divorces, some financial difficulties, and even some addiction issues. But as we sat at lunch he said unequivocally that he was there by the "grace of God and the prayers of a steadfast, loving mother."

In recent years, I've heard from Dotty about how both of her children have been there for her. She's been a widow for over twenty years. Her daughter Debbie is always quick to lend her mom a hand or travel with her to an event. John has been invaluable when it comes to making repairs on her home or overseeing a home project. One day, Dotty and I met for lunch halfway between our homes and after eating we went back to her car to pray, as is our custom. We walked up to a car I didn't recognize. She had driven a nice, burgundy Buick for as long as I could remember. Parked before my eyes was a beautiful, new silver CTS Cadillac.

"Wow," I said. "When did you get this?" I asked.

"Oh honey! Can you believe it? John bought it for me!" she said. She went on to say how one Mother's Day he just showed up and said, "Mom, I think it's time for you to get a new car. Let's go car shopping." Before she could object, he insisted and they were out the door. To her surprise, in her driveway sat her brand new car.

"At eighty one years old, it's more than I needed, that's for sure. But I sure do feel safe in it and I have that service that will respond to me in my car if I'm ever in need. I just couldn't believe it, honey, when he showed up with it. He's been so good to me," she said gratefully.

What a blessing John was to his mother! He was putting into practice what it means biblically to honor our parents. I jokingly suggested that I might want to pass on this example to my daughters just in case they might need some ideas as I approach my latter years!

Honoring may not always occur in the same form, but in this section, we are going to talk about five principles for honoring your parents in adulthood. We are going to see that while the particular expressions of honor may vary, they are rooted in scriptural principles that stand the test of time and extend to all cultures.

Here are the five principles, simply stated:

- Show *kindness* and *respect* for what they provided (1 Timothy 5:4)
- Speak *truth in love* when necessary (Ephesians 4:15)
- Set a *pattern of loving behavior* for your own children (1 Corinthians 11:1)
- Seek to *settle issues* as much as is possible (Romans 12:18)
- Submit to God's *authority* and *sovereignty* in your life (Psalm 139)

Chapter 9

SHOW KINDNESS AND RESPECT

Do you remember the interview with Dr. Sunukjian in which we talked about the "legitimate debt" we owe to our parents? Honoring our parents is demonstrated in part through our acknowledgment of what our parents provided for us as children. According to 1 Timothy 5:4, honor may also include providing financial care for our aging or widowed parent when necessary: "But if a widow has children or grandchildren, these should learn first of all to put their religion into practice by caring for their own family and so repaying their parents and grandparents, for this is pleasing to God" (NIV).

The word "repaying" in this verse is used in the positive sense of returning the good which children and grandchildren received in childhood from their parents and grandparents. A similar verse in James tells us that the kind of religion God accepts and finds "pure and faultless" demonstrates itself by "[looking] after orphans and widows in their distress" (James 1:27 NIV). Further, you may recall Jesus' indictment of the Pharisees for their failure to show honor to their parents through financial provision. They instead clung to a tradition-based loophole that allowed them to shirk their responsibility to their parents, claiming that money that should have been used to assist their parents was "devoted to God" (Mark 7:9–13 niv). It's clear that one way we honor is by "giving back" through caring for our aging parents or contributing financially to their care.

Another very practical way we can show honor is simply to be present with them. We make them a priority by showing care and concern for where they are in life, and at times we offer our assistance. We may accompany them to doctors' appointments, take them grocery shopping, or invite them over for dinner once a month.

I have a friend who makes dinner every Monday night for her widowed mother and her widower father-in-law. She provides them with both an evening out of their own homes and an opportunity to spend quality time with their grandchildren on a regular basis. Also, by establishing a regular weekly visit, she was able to set up a buffer in her relationship with her mother, with whom she has had difficulty establishing healthy boundaries.

After my stepfather died, my mother's purpose in life seemed to diminish. Due to my stepfather's physical condition prior to his death, he had required my mother's fulltime attention. She made little time for herself or for maintaining friendships. As a result, she suffered intense loneliness and her physical condition deteriorated. In the space of four years she had two knee replacements and developed stage four ovarian cancer. She underwent extensive surgery and was hospitalized for over three weeks. During that time, my younger brother and I coordinated our daily visits. I drove seventy five miles a day to visit in the morning and he came late in the afternoon.

It was a very stressful time. I discovered a level of grief that I had never before faced. My mother was very weak and helpless. She needed me to do some things for her that she couldn't do for herself. I was brushing her hair, helping her eat, and being her advocate with the nursing staff.

After two weeks, I was exhausted and feeling a little resentful. How was it that I was caring for and advocating for my mother when she had not done so for me when I was a child? Where had she been when I needed her most? It brought back some deep feelings of childhood aloneness and helplessness. God was inviting me to a deeper level of healing and He was using this experience to accomplish His purposes.

I'm so grateful for friends who could support me, pray for me, and help me process what I was feeling. Being honest and vulnerable with trusted friends helped me walk through another layer of grief. And as I poured out my heart before God and asked Him for the grace I needed to be present for my mom, He was there to offer an abundant provision. At several points, neither my brother nor I thought my mother would survive, but God was gracious and she has been cancer free for over four years.

Since my stepfather's death six years ago, my mom and I have grown considerably closer. We enjoy each other and appreciate our similarities in personality. We have laughed and cried, exchanged stories, shared regrets, and deepened our friendship. I am so thankful that God gave me these years with my mom. He has taught me a great deal about what it means to demonstrate kindness to parents in spite of their failures.

For some who are reading, this is a tough pill to swallow. I understand. I did not come to this place instantly. It takes willingness and it takes time. I wasn't going to try to fake it. I knew if I was to come to a place of honoring my parents, it had to be genuine. I also knew I could not muster it up on my own. I needed God and others to help walk me through the process.

I remember sitting with a brother and sister whose parents had been raging alcoholics. They talked about how little food and clothing they had growing up because every paycheck went to support their parents' alcohol abuse. They remember going to school hungry and finding ways to spend time with friends and their families on the weekend in order to eat.

Extreme situations such as this may limit or rule out certain ways of showing honor to our parents. It may not be the wisest course of action or the best stewardship to provide money to parents who have a history of drug or alcohol abuse, or who have demonstrated careless financial behavior. There are, however, ways to show kindness and respect to parents whose negligence had profound impact in our lives. We choose to look for and appreciate any ways in which our parents cared for our needs, even amidst horrific circumstances that caused us grief or injury. Remember, this does not mean we pretend or gloss over reality. It means that we acknowledge our parents' efforts of sustaining our life even in the most basic ways of providing food, shelter, medical care, clothing, or a roof over our heads. For many of us, our parents did so much more than provide the basics; those additional things are the fodder for our expressions of gratitude.

I remember in my own life there was a time that all I could focus on was the way my life had been ravaged by my stepfather's abuse and my mother's lack of protection. It was an important part of the grieving process to identify and enumerate the multiple layers of loss in my life in order to grieve properly, and ultimately forgive. As Drs. Cloud and Townsend put it,

> To truly forgive, you cannot deny or try to overlook what happened. You must acknowledge the offense in order to be free. And just because you forgive does not mean that the feelings will automatically disappear. When you do your best to forgive, don't be troubled if you still experience anger or sadness when reminded of something. It doesn't mean you haven't truly forgiven.[1]

When we properly grieve through our losses and work through forgiveness, it grants us the ability to shift our focus. There came a time when I took stock of the good things that I had been afforded throughout my childhood by my parents: braces for crooked teeth; help with school projects; a good work ethic; instruction in household chores; habits of orderliness and proper hygiene; and a myriad of other things for which I am grateful today. I was genuinely able to express my gratitude to my parents because I took the time to consider thoughtfully their contributions to my upbringing.

We demonstrate kindness and respect in our dealings with our parents and do not make it our aim to demean or discredit them in front of others. We don't speak to them or about them in a malicious or disrespectful tone. We recognize that all of us are sinful human beings with strengths and weaknesses, good and bad character traits, and we are all in need of grace and forgiveness. All of this is what Jesus died for on the cross. He died for the sins I commit and the sins committed against me and He has the power to redeem it all as we collaborate with Him in the process of restoration.

The pathway toward this acceptance is lengthier for some than it is for others. God knows our hearts and the details of our lives and through His Spirit He can empower us to show kindness and respect to our parents. I realized early on in my own process of healing that God is a God who redeems everything. There is nothing that we have endured that God cannot use in our lives to bring about His good purpose. (Romans 8:28). When we as adults show kindness and respect to our parents, regardless of the ways they may have been dishonorable, we honor God who establishes all those in authority over us (Romans 13:1–2).

Chapter 10

SPEAK THE TRUTH IN LOVE

One of my favorite verses in Scripture concerning relationships reads: "Speaking the truth in love, [we] may grow up in all things into Him who is the head—Christ" (Ephesians 4:15 NKJV). In my counseling practice, I often quote this verse to couples because I think it speaks to the heart of what marriage is designed by God to do—help us grow up into maturity in Christ. I frequently see marriages in which one spouse loves giving the truth but has a difficult time receiving it, while the other is reluctant to speak the truth because of fear of rejection or abandonment.

My family knows that I am a "truth giver" by nature, but I must confess that sometimes it has been difficult hearing the truth, especially from my children. One morning, when our youngest daughter Kellie was fifteen, she and I were having a conversation in the kitchen about her needing money for some future school activities. She commented that she wished some babysitting opportunities would present themselves so she could earn some cash. I agreed. No sooner had we discussed this than the telephone rang. Kellie answered the phone and I heard her say, "Oh, thank you so much Mrs. MacKenzie, I would love to babysit for you, but I've already made plans for this Saturday evening." I was standing in the kitchen as this conversation ensued, mouthing the words, "Take the job!" Kellie politely thanked her again, gave her the name of a friend who might be available, and hung up the phone.

I immediately said, "Kellie, we just talked about your need for money and you got a call. How could you not take the job?"

Calmly she said, "Mom, I already made plans with my friends for Saturday and I don't feel right about canceling."

"Well, it sure seems to me like that was an answer to your prayers—I think you should have taken the job. But it's your decision, you can do what you want," I said shaking my head in disbelief.

Kellie looked at me pointedly, but respectfully said, "Mom, I hate when you do that. You put a lot of pressure on me to do what you want me to do and then you tag on 'But, go ahead and do what you want.' It makes me feel like it's really not my decision." Just about that time, our seventeen-year-old daughter Heather walked in the kitchen having overheard our interaction. She chimed in, "Yeah, I hate that too, Mom."

I wish I could tell you that I immediately embraced their words with gratitude. I didn't. In fact, that night as we all sat around the dinner table there was little conversation between us. My husband Don was not privy to what had transpired and couldn't figure out why the silence.

As I sat there, I heard the Spirit's conviction in my heart say, "They're right, you know." I protested initially, rationalizing that Kellie really should have taken the job that God had so graciously provided! Then rather sheepishly after dinner, I said, "Girls, we need to talk. Let's go sit in the family room." We gathered there, my two girls sitting next to each other on the couch and me on the chopping block across from them.

"Girls, you both are telling me the same thing and what that tells me is that you're not crazy. You've talked to me about this before and I'm obviously still pressuring you to do things my way. This is a character problem in me and I know it's something that needs to change. I want you to know that I'm sorry and I don't want to do this to either of you anymore. I know I will probably not change overnight, so I give you permission to remind me respectfully when I do it again. I'm really sorry and promise you that I'm going to work on this with God's help. Would you forgive me?"

They accepted my apology graciously and then looked at each other with a smile as if to say, "Finally, one for the kids!" I remember sitting in our family room after that exchange, shedding a few tears of gratitude. I thanked the Lord for allowing me to experience with my children something I never experienced with my parents. God was graciously doing a new work in our family.

Speaking the truth in love to your parents may not be as easy as it sounds, especially if as a child you were not encouraged to speak up or allowed to have a different opinion. In some families it is deemed disrespectful or dishonoring to express a different viewpoint even when children are well into adulthood and even when done in a respectful manner. "But many parents can and do change when the old routine is stopped, so if you can grow and encourage your parents to grow along with you, then you can communicate on a more honest and authentic level."[1]

When Generations Gap

I remember a conversation I had with my mother a number of years ago about my daughter Heather's high school graduation. I came home from work one evening and Don told me that my mother had phoned to say they'd received Heather's graduation announcement. Don recounted their brief conversation and I knew what was coming. Mom talked to Don about my stepfather's latest health concern and I knew she was setting the stage for not attending Heather's graduation. This was an all too familiar pattern. As long as I could remember, my mom had used my stepfather as an excuse for avoiding responsibilities to other family members. I knew I needed to pray before I returned her call and I asked the Lord to help me be loving but truthful.

I phoned her back later that evening and the conversation steered toward how concerned she was about my stepfather. She went into a detailed account of what she had to do for him every day. She then added that she wasn't sure she'd be able to come to Heather's graduation. I was hurt and disappointed because I knew she had recently attended another event and arranged to have a good friend over to care for my dad while she was away for the evening. I also knew my dad's condition was not serious at that time, and my mom was using his health as her excuse for not coming. I listened to all she had to say and then said, "Mom, it sounds like you're telling me all of this to say you're not coming to Heather's graduation. I understand Dad has health issues and that you're concerned. But Mom, I'm going to be disappointed if you don't come to your granddaughter's high school graduation."

Immediately her walls of defense went up. Angrily she said, "I would never have spoken to *my* mother that way." In a very low, kind voice I said, "Mom, I'm just sharing with you how I will feel if you don't come to Heather's graduation. I've never asked you to attend anything else that my girls have ever been involved in, but it would be nice for Heather to have her grandmother there."

Since anger didn't work to change my mind or make me apologize for expressing myself, she turned to tears. "You have no idea how hard it is on me to care for your Dad. I can't believe you would talk to me this way."

"Mom, there's nothing wrong with expressing my feelings to you. If you decide not to come, I will not be mad at you. I will still love you, but I will be disappointed."

By this time she was desperate. I heard my stepfather yelling at me in the background and in a tearful burst she said, "You have no idea how hard my life is. I would never have spoken to my mother like this!" And then I heard a click. She'd hung up on me.

I was stunned. My mother had never hung up on me before. I was very familiar with the pattern of anger followed by a tearful ploy, but I wasn't prepared for being hung up on. Then, as usual I plunged into guilt. Had I crossed the line? Had I been disrespectful or dishonoring? Should I have just kept my mouth shut and not shared my feelings? I felt an immediate urge to call her back, let her off the hook from attending the graduation, and apologize for sharing my feelings. Instead, I prayed and felt led to call my friend Dotty. I needed feedback from a godly woman near my mom's age. I knew Dotty would speak the truth to me and give me wise counsel. I was pretty sure she would confirm my inclination to call my mom back and apologize.

I called Dotty and recounted the phone conversation with my mom and asked for her wisdom.

"I'm wondering if I should call her back and apologize. What do you think the Lord would want me to do?" I asked sincerely.

"Honey," she said lovingly but emphatically, "I don't think you should call her back. She hung up on you and I think you should wait for her to make the call."

"Really? Do you think I was wrong for sharing my feelings of disappointment with her?" I asked.

"Absolutely not. If the same situation took place with my daughter Debbie she would have let me have it. It's not too much to ask that a grandmother attend her grandchild's high school graduation. It sounds to me like you were kind, but truthful. I think your mom is probably feeling guilty. She knows how she has let you down over the years and she's feeling bad. It is okay for her to sit with that for a while. Honey, let the Holy Spirit use this in her life right now. Don't call. Just wait and pray and see what happens."

I was a bit surprised by Dotty's counsel, but I decided to wait and pray. Two weeks went by before the phone rang. My mom's first words were, "I can't believe you haven't called to find out about your Dad's test results." I said, "Mom, you hung up on me, so I decided to wait for a while." Immediately her defenses were in full swing again and it was an instant replay of our last conversation. No matter what I said, she would not accept that feelings of disappointment or hurt should ever be shared in a relationship with a parent. Finally, toward the end of the conversation she said she was working on finding care for my dad and that she would try to be at the graduation. I apologized to her for assuming she wasn't coming and I voiced my appreciation for her making the effort to be there. She did attend and it turned out to be a nice celebration.

Thankfully, our relationship has grown since then, and although my mom still has difficulty when I share feelings with her, we've been able to weather the storms and work to build a healthier relationship with one another.

Time-Tempered Truth

I've noticed something lately when sitting in various waiting rooms reading the magazines provided. There usually seem to be several articles about celebrities who are speaking "truth" about their experiences as children.

I read an article recently about Brooke Shields who, "after growing up in a 'toxic' environment"[2] is making peace with her mother—and giving her own girls the childhood she never had. Another article detailed Tatum O'Neal's struggle with addictions and her recent reconnection with her famous father, Ryan O'Neal, who abandoned her as a child. Ashley Judd's 2011 memoir revealed abuse in her background and long-standing family dysfunction.

What I found most intriguing was that all of these women, now in their forties, were attempting to come to grips with issues from their childhoods that had never been openly talked about. Each of them seemed to desire some sort of reconciliation or forgiveness that would allow them to move on in life. All of these women expressed a passion for helping their own children or other children avoid similar experiences. Their hope was that they could offer their children something better than what they had experienced. Part of their process included speaking the truth about what happened, as well as reaching a point of graciousness toward their parents' own struggles.

I think time often tempers us. This is especially true when we have our own children and recognize the delicate and arduous nature of parenting. Speaking the truth in love is most helpful when seasoned with grace. The goal is to help the recipient grow into maturity by facing reality. As in the case with my daughters, the information they provided me left me with an opportunity to change. We are not responsible for the outcome of speaking the truth, but we are responsible for our method and our motive. If you're in a situation with your parents where you are wondering about whether or not to speak the truth about something, it will be beneficial to all if you are able to sort through the issues, examine your motives, and talk with an objective, qualified person about the method that would be most helpful in your individual situation.

For many families, unhealthy relationship patterns die hard. And some families never change. As adults, we each have an individual responsibility to follow God's guidelines when it comes to relationships. We're to speak the truth in love while at the same time maintaining respectfulness and gentleness. We will all fall short at times and we all need God's grace. It's no wonder that the apostle Paul admonishes us in Colossians 3:13 with these words: "Bear with each other and forgive one another if any of you has a grievance against someone. Forgive as the Lord forgave you" (NIV).

Chapter 11

SET A PATTERN OF LOVING BEHAVIOR

Do you remember a time when you were driving in your car with your young children in the back seat when someone cut you off and you blurted out some choice words about the other driver? Do you also remember driving around town a few days later and hearing your four-year-old utter those same words? Most of us have experienced something like this with our children. We are setting a pattern of behavior for them whether we are aware of it or not.

I was well into my parenting years before I thought about the fact that my children were observing and learning from my relationship with my parents. I knew the old adage about significant things being "caught" rather than "taught," but I hadn't mentally connected this principle with my everyday dealings with my parents. I'm so grateful to God that He was overseeing my steps even though I was not consciously aware of the impact I was making.

I remember one Christmas when my youngest daughter Kellie was a teenager. We were out shopping and I was looking for gifts for my parents. Although we didn't spend Christmas Day with them, we always made the hour drive to their home sometime prior to Christmas to visit and spend the afternoon. Kellie commented how Grandma always gave each of them a Christmas card with $10 enclosed.

I'll never forget Kellie cocking her head to one side and with a puzzled look on her face asking, "Mom, what do *you* get from Grandma and Grandpa at Christmas?" I said rather matter-of-factly, "Nothing, honey. My parents stopped giving me gifts when I moved out of their house at twenty one." Kellie was shocked. "What do you mean? They don't give you anything, even for your birthday?" "No, honey they don't, but Grandma always sends me a very nice card."

Kellie couldn't quite grasp this. She was full of questions as to why this was the way it was and why I continued to buy gifts for them for Mother's and Father's Day, their birthdays, and Christmas. Kellie and I resumed our shopping, but I could tell something registered in her heart. I think it was a mixture of sadness and a bit of admiration. She knew that it was only by God's grace that I had been able to move beyond childhood losses and extend love and honor toward my parents.

Over the years, I've heard countless stories of others who've given far more sacrificially than I to their parents. One young woman I know whose mother had multiple marriages and live-in boyfriends, drank excessively, and failed to protect her daughter from the sexual advances of multiple partners, took time away from her own family to provide daily care for her mother who is at the time of writing dying of cancer. My young friend admits that it has not been easy, especially because to this day her mother is in denial about all that went on in their home growing up. She confessed that sometimes she dreads getting a call from her mother. But then she prays and asks God for strength. Knowing there is no one else in her mother's life who can extend to her the love of Jesus, she goes and offers what help she can.

Many of us have not had parents who were good role models, but by

God's grace we can live life differently than our parents did. The apostle Paul had something to say about how to do this: "Follow God's example, therefore, as dearly loved children and walk in the way of love, just as Christ loved us and gave himself up for us as a fragrant offering and sacrifice to God" (Ephesians 5:1–2 NIV).

I've heard this verse for years, but recently I came to understand it in a new way. Paul admonishes us to be "imitators of God as dearly loved children." Paul was tapping into a principle of human relationships. We tend to repeat what we experience. He is saying you are dearly loved children of God who can imitate Him because of your relational experience of His love for you. It hit me. I could imitate God by living a life of love, not because I grew up in a home in which I was perfectly loved, but because I have experienced what it is to be a dearly loved child of God.

This isn't to say that we don't need human role models to help us in the process of learning. Cloud and Townsend write, "We cannot do what we have never seen done. We need models to show us how. God designed humans with a need to see others first do what they need to learn, and then to internalize that modeling and be able to repeat it."[1] The apostle Paul understood this when he wrote, "Follow my example, as I follow the example of Christ" (1 Corinthians 11:1 NIV). Later, he admonished his protégé to "entrust to reliable people" (2 Timothy 2:2 NIV) the things he'd heard from Paul and to "keep . . . the pattern of sound teaching" (2 Timothy 1:13 NIV).

An Example Well Worth Repeating

One day I had a conversation with my mom about my grandfather. Luther Elmer Garrett was born in Arkansas in 1889. On December 12, 1907, the year of Oklahoma statehood, he married my grandmother, Rosie Nell Fisher, in Ada, Oklahoma. My grandpa was nineteen years old and my grandma was fourteen. My grandpa worked for the Oklahoma-Central Railroad for twenty six years until it was closed in 1942, and then moved his family to California. My grandparents had nine children. Their oldest daughter died at the age of five. My mother, the youngest girl, had three older brothers, three older sisters, and a younger brother.

We saw my grandparents often as children, but by the time I was born they seemed really old. I have a few memories of staying at their home as a little girl, playing in their yard, eating my favorite caramel cake that my grandma made from scratch, attending tent revival meetings with my grandparents, and having church services in my grandparent's home.

Grandma was a "preacher" of sorts and often would have twenty to thirty people in her home on a Sunday morning. She would play the piano and we all sang gospel hymns like "The Old Rugged Cross" and "Rock of Ages." Grandma would then stand up and deliver a Bible message. I can still hear the "Amens" and "Hallelujahs" that accompanied her impassioned orations.

In 1972, the year I graduated from high school, my grandmother suffered a heart attack and so my grandparents sold their home and moved back to Oklahoma to be near their other children. My grandma died of cancer in December of 1978 at the age of eighty five. My grandparents were married for seventy one years.

In 1985, my mother and stepfather were taking a trip across country and planned to visit my grandpa who by this time was living with one of my aunts. My aunt asked my mom if Grandpa could go home with them for a month so she and her husband could take a needed vacation. My mother agreed and brought my grandpa back to California.

According to my mom, grandpa never wanted to return to Oklahoma. But grandma could be a very strong and persuasive woman and so they made the move. I think those traits must be genetic. My mom became somewhat concerned for my grandpa's overall health the first week he was with us. He was ninety six at the time but still very sharp and witty. He told my mom that he needed cataract surgery but my aunt was afraid to take him into Oklahoma City to have it done. Within a week of his arrival, my mom made an appointment for him and the surgery was a success. It significantly improved his vision, allowing him to resume riding his adult tricycle around the neighborhood until he was ninety eight years old. What was originally intended as a one-month visit turned into a four-year living arrangement.

One day when my aunt from Oklahoma called to talk with my grandpa, my mother overheard him say, "I'm not coming back unless they kick me out." For two years, Grandpa lived with my parents. When we visited, he would always recite a poem he'd learned as a boy, sing an old gospel hymn, or recite his favorite psalm—Psalm 1—in its entirety.

Now, years later as I talked with my mom about my grandfather, I asked, "When did you have to put Grandpa into the nursing home?"

"That was in 1987. That was the hardest thing I ever had to do," she said tearfully. "Papa got to the point that he couldn't walk very well and neither your father nor I could lift him. He couldn't ride his tricycle anymore and it just became too difficult to care for him on a daily basis."

"How long was he in there?" I asked.

"Two years. Do you remember visiting him there?" she asked.

"I sure do. I remember we brought our girls up to see him and he still remembered coming to our house for a barbecue several years earlier. He sure stayed sharp until the end," I said fondly.

"Yes, and they loved him at the nursing home. When I put him in there I signed up to volunteer daily for three hours. I know it made Papa feel better that he could see me around there. It was hard each day when I'd go to his room, kiss him on the cheek, and say, 'I'll see you tomorrow, Papa.'"

Two years later, my mom hosted a hundredth birthday celebration for Grandpa. She called the local newspaper and they did an article on him. Just four months later Grandpa died of pneumonia.

As my mom and I were reminiscing, there was only one reference to her life growing up. She commented on how life was very different then because they were poor. She went to work at the age of fourteen just to help supplement the family income because my grandpa was unable to work due to his impaired vision and arthritis. Although my mom is now eighty three, I could hear in her voice a longing for her parents. Even at her age, she missed them.

When I hung up the phone, I couldn't help but reflect on our conversation. I thought about my mom caring for my grandpa and how it warmed my heart. I felt a deep admiration for my mom who modeled honoring her father long before it ever mattered to me.

I thought about one of my most treasured possessions. It's a letter I received from my grandma in 1978 just months before she passed away. In it she wrote, "We remember when you preached at our house. Papa believes you was called to preach." She was referring to a time that I stayed at their home as a little girl. On one Sunday morning I was invited to "deliver a message" when the scheduled preacher became ill. To this day, each time I stand before the women in my Bible study, teach at a conference, or speak at a retreat, those words echo in my mind. It's a blessing of my heritage. It is the evidence of the sovereign hand of God at work to bring about redemption before the story had been written.

I thought about the fervent prayers of my grandparents and how God promises that the prayers of the righteous are "powerful and effective" (James 5:16 NIV).

I learned a great deal that day just by asking my mother about my grandfather. I realized my life had become richer simply through having shown interest in someone she loved.

Setting an example of loving and honoring your parents is an investment that pays compound interest. You are blessed with the joy of obedience to God while at the same time cultivating a legacy that will live on in your children long after you have passed on. Wouldn't it be a blessing in eternity to hear your Master say, "Your legacy of honoring your parents continued in each successive generation until I came back for My church. Well done, good and faithful servant."

> *"How you honor or dishonor your parents will be noticed and absorbed by the next generation."*[2]

Chapter 12

SEEK TO SETTLE ISSUES

Several years ago I received a call from my half-brother who is nine years younger than I am. My parents had been in a terrible automobile accident and my mother had to be cut out of the car with the Jaws of Life. They were both hospitalized but suffered only mild injuries due to the fact that they were wearing their seatbelts. I'll never forget visiting them in the hospital. I stood between them, arms extended, holding each of their hands as they lay in their hospital beds. I prayed for them and with them, thanking God for His mercy in sparing their lives.

As I stood there, I uttered a silent prayer of thanksgiving to God: *Lord, thank you that it's clean between us.* I dealt with the issues of growing up in my family long before this incident occurred and as a result there was no "unfinished business" to complicate this delicate situation. I drove home from the hospital that day thanking God that had my parents died that day, there would have been no regrets. By God's grace, I had followed His prompting over the years, seeking to settle issues and God had brought about reconciliation.

But what about the times when reconciliation seems to stay just out of reach? And what might it look like to honor parents who refuse to admit difficult truths about past failures, thus leaving issues perpetually unresolved? In what follows, I outline some scriptural insights about the value of *seeking* to settle issues, even when reconciliation remains elusive.

"As Far as It Depends On You"

Romans 12:18 exhorts us: "If it is possible, as far as it depends on you, live at peace with everyone" (NIV). I think that short verse has always intrigued me because it is one of the rare commands in Scripture with a built-in caveat. "If possible *(and it may not be)*, as far as it depends on you *(you're responsible only to do your part)*, live at peace with everyone."

The context of this verse is how believers are to relate with unbelievers, but the principle holds true within families as well. The word translated "peace" in this verse carries the notion of "bringing peace" or "reconciling."[1] One commentator writes, "Believers should do their utmost to seek reconciliation."[2]

Reconciliation means to "settle or resolve differences" or "to bring harmony."[3] Dr. David Stoop writes this about reconciliation and forgiveness:

> Forgiveness is a singular activity. It is something I do within me, and I don't need the other person to participate in the process for me to forgive. Reconciliation is a bilateral process, requiring the participation of both parties. For there to be genuine reconciliation, I need to forgive and the other person needs to show godly sorrow over what he or she has done. Forgiveness is required of us as believers, but reconciliation is optional and depends on the attitude of the offender.[4]

Seeking to settle issues or bring reconciliation is not always possible. I have known many people who were committed to bringing resolution and healing to their families, only to be rebuffed or criticized for "stirring up trouble."

I think the apostle Paul must have known that in some situations reconciliation may not be possible. Even though there is no indication in Scripture, I've wondered if Paul himself might have had some personal experience with failing to reach reconciliation. Some questions came to my mind: Were Paul's parents alive when he persecuted the early Jewish Christians for their adoption of the gospel? How did Paul handle family members who wanted nothing to do with him after his newfound faith? Did his parents and family suffer ostracism by the Jewish leaders in their hometown due to Paul's conversion? Would his parents have said Paul was dishonoring them by laying hold of this faith that seemed to contradict all they held dear?

We know little about Paul's family and nothing of their reaction to his conversion.[5] We know that Paul's father was a prominent Pharisee in their hometown of Tarsus. Paul himself was educated in Jerusalem in the strictest rabbinic tradition. When Paul requested letters from the high priest in Jerusalem permitting him to pursue his obsession with apprehending and annihilating all those who followed the new Messiah, he must have been something of a local hero to many of his fellow Jews.[6]

Following his conversion on the Damascus road, Paul spent time in Arabia, Damascus, and Jerusalem, before eventually returning to Tarsus.[7] No doubt it shocked relatives, friends, and neighbors that their hometown hero was now passionately proclaiming the faith he had once tried to destroy. I wonder if Paul attempted to reconcile with members of his family, only to experience resistance and hostility. I wonder if maybe he wrote Romans 12:18 with his personal experiences in mind. Paul says to us, "Do your best to bring about reconciliation, but know that it is not always within your ability or control." If we have done all we can do to bring about reconciliation with our parents, we can be assured that God honors our efforts, even in the absence of a fully realized reconciliation.

Settling Issues while Preserving the Truth

Seeking to settle issues means we deal with reality from a loving perspective. We attempt to deal with what is true from a place of humility and forgiveness without compromising truth. One of my favorite quotes comes from a man named Charles Sell who grew up in an alcoholic home. Inadvertently, he found himself repeating some relational patterns with his own children and discovered that he needed to address the truth of his own background if he was to make the necessary changes to break the sin cycle in his family. He writes: "[But] facing the facts is not betraying your family. Truth is the issue, not love or loyalty. Love covers a multitude of sins, but it should not distort them. Our objective is not to find fault, but to find help; and we are not out to accuse and attack our parents, but to understand ourselves better."[8]

Seeking to settle issues has at its core a desire to have an adult-to-adult relationship with your parents that is steeped in both grace and truth. This may mean sitting down with your parents and discussing the issues that helped shape your life, both positive and negative. It might include affirming all the ways in which you understand how difficult it is to be a parent and how you have learned by experience that raising children is quite challenging. It may involve asking questions about what was going on in their lives and hearts at a particular time in your childhood in order to gain a greater understanding of their struggles. It may require sharing some of the hurt and disappointment you experienced as a child as a result of some of their choices. But it will always include a spirit of humility and a deep desire to bring reconciliation and healing to the relationship through forgiveness.

Chapter 13

SUBMIT TO GOD'S AUTHORITY AND SOVEREIGNTY

I have struggled with authority figures most of my life. I think it is a result of growing up in a family where authority was misused and unreasonable. For the most part, the struggle was an internal one and it did not show up externally until adolescence. I was a model student in school and was very well liked by my teachers and classmates. Because I was vocal about my faith in high school, I wanted to be a good example of what it meant to follow Jesus. I didn't drink or go to parties. And I never defied those in authority—except once.

In my freshman year of high school my Spanish teacher's name was Señora Rivera. She was tough. I took Spanish in elementary school and in both years in junior high school and I had done well. Señora Rivera was probably in her late fifties or early sixties and from all appearances she was not happy in her job. I and my fellow classmates, most of whom were honor students, knew every time we walked into class that we weren't going to measure up. Señora Rivera had a volatile temper and it seemed like no effort was good enough to warrant her pleasure.

I don't know why, but one day I'd had enough. I didn't go into class with any agenda, but when Señora Rivera was not pleased with our recitation of the homework, I could feel my irritation rising. When she screamed, "Get out your books and study the lesson until you can get it right!" everyone did as they were told in complete silence, except me. I sat quietly at my desk with my book unopened. After a few minutes passed, Señora Rivera looked up and said to me, "Señorita Matthews, why are you just sitting there not doing your work?" I remember thinking, *This is it! It's my opportunity to say what we have all been feeling for months.*

"I'm not doing my work because it seems like whatever we do in here it's never good enough for you anyway!" I said. I happened to look across the room at one of my girlfriend's faces just as I finished my sentence. Her look of horrified disbelief seemed to say, *What have you just done?*

Señora Rivera stood up from behind her desk, eyes ablaze, and ordered me to report to the principal's office immediately. To be honest, I felt ashamed and liberated at the same time! Someone needed to speak the truth and end the tyranny. I don't remember much of the conversation with the principal, but he was a reasonable man who knew my track record. He told me that I would not be allowed back into class until a parent and I had a conference with Señora Rivera.

Surprisingly, I wasn't that concerned about my parents' reaction to this incident because my stepfather had drummed into me the importance of standing up for what is right. He often told a story about being picked on as a little boy and how my grandfather made him go find the boy and "finish what the boy had started."

When I told my mother what had happened that day, she was less than pleased and announced that I would have to tell my stepfather at dinner what had transpired. I genuinely thought my dad would be somewhat proud of me for what I had done. I had miscalculated badly! My stepfather was furious at me and told me I had better never challenge authority like that again or I would live to regret it.

My mom and I went to the conference and I apologized to Señora Rivera. Something unexpected happened. For the first time ever, I saw a soft side of this angry woman. She shared how she lost her seven-year-old daughter to an illness and that she had never really gotten over it. I told her how sorry I was for challenging her authority in front of the other students and that it would never happen again. I can't explain it, but from that time until the end of the school year, Señora Rivera was a different woman. She was less exacting and more encouraging to us as a class. She showed patience and understanding. She even seemed to like me.

Of course, it wasn't until years later that I understood the root of my untimely outburst. I was rebelling against everything that was taking place in my home—the abuse, the unreasonable expectations, the criticism, the hypocrisy, the cruelty, the injustice. I understood a little of what Señora Rivera must have felt when life served up circumstances that seemed so unfair and unwarranted.

Submitting to God's authority and sovereignty is a lifelong process. It comes easier for some than for others, depending on one's background. It occurred to me early in the process of writing this book how pivotal the issue of authority is in our life. No matter what our situation, chosen vocation, or living condition we are all subject to authority.

"We were not created to be our own final authority. As adults, we all have to defer and submit, at some point, to other authorities in our lives. From God on down to bosses and supervisors and spouses, we need to respect someone."[1]

God in His infinite wisdom placed us in families to learn this most crucial aspect of living productively in the world. And not just in the physical world, but in the spiritual realm as well.

The Bible has a lot to say about authority. A scriptural principle relevant for the topic of this book is that God has established all authority, whether governmental or familial. *Exsousia,* the Greek word commonly translated as "authority" in the New Testament, means "the right to exercise power."[2] God placed us within families with parents to whom God has given the right to exercise power over us. Some parents misuse and abuse that power, while others diligently try to exercise that authority with wisdom and humility. What I realized in my own life as a parent is that as diligent as I tried to be in exercising loving authority over our children, I fell short. We all do. There is not a parent who has ever walked this earth who has done his or her job perfectly.

As we talk about what it looks like to honor our parents in adulthood, we are faced with this reality: God chose our parents. He determined in His sovereignty the family in which we were placed. This reality hit me squarely early in my recovery process; God *chose* my parents. God knew all the events that would transpire in my life. He knew everything, and yet, this is where God placed me. I wrestled through these issues years ago. How could a God who loves me have allowed these things to occur? Why didn't He intervene in my life? Couldn't God have placed me in another home with different parents who would have loved me and protected me? How am I ever to learn to trust God as Father, given my background?

I candidly share that recovery process in my book *Door of Hope.* God tenderly walked me through the process of accepting His authority in my life. It did not happen overnight but was a process of learning to trust Him day by day and yield to His right to rule in my life. I love Beth Moore's reminder in *Breaking Free*: "The One who has a right to rule is also the One whose rule is right."[3]

God not only has the right to rule, He is sovereign over all the events that transpire in our lives. Psalm 139:16 gives me comfort as I survey the events of my life: "All the days ordained for me were written in your book before one of them came to be" (NIV). Nothing takes God by surprise. He is not limited by the sinfulness of humanity, but He sovereignly works to bring about His good purposes in the lives of His children. When I see my parents and the events of my life from the vantage point of this truth, I'm able to say "yes" to God's sovereignty in my life.

Do you remember earlier in the book when I shared about how I accepted Jesus into my life at the age of ten? It was January 17, 1965, at an evening service at our church. I raised my hand that evening and asked Jesus to come into my heart. I'll never forget the woman who counseled me in the prayer room afterwards telling me, "The angels are rejoicing in heaven over you and the decision you've made." For a ten-year-old little girl who didn't have a lot of people rejoicing over her, that was huge. Afterwards, when my sister and I left the church service later than expected, we found our stepfather waiting impatiently in the car. Anger in his voice, he said, "Where have you girls been? I've been sitting here waiting for you!" Just having heard that the angels were rejoicing, I said with bright-eyed excitement, "Dad, I just asked Jesus into my heart tonight!" Scowling, he snapped back, "Why didn't you wait until your mother and I were here?" As soon as he spoke those words, the angels stopped singing and a little girl's heart shattered.

I repeat this story because it is integral to the story I am about to tell you. Fast-forward forty one years. I got a call one winter day that my stepfather had died after a bout of pneumonia. I left work immediately and made arrangements to travel to my parents' home to help my mom with the funeral arrangements.

In the course of discussing the funeral service, I told my mom that I would like to say a few words at the service. My mom was agreeable, but when I voiced that request to my half brother, he dubiously asked, "What are you planning to say?" I can't blame him for asking. I'm sure the doubt I heard in his voice was not totally unwarranted given my outspoken nature. I said reassuringly, "Don't worry, Bro. It will not be anything you have to worry about. It will be short—two, three minutes at the most, and it will be kind." I could hear the sigh of relief on the other end of the phone.

Prior to the service, both of my daughters called to say they wanted to attend the service to support their grandmother and me. My oldest daughter Heather, who is quite outspoken herself, said to me, "Mom, if they start talking about what a great guy Grandpa was at his funeral, I'm getting up and walking out. I don't know how you can speak at his funeral anyway, after everything he did to you."

I said, "Heather, I doubt there will be anyone else speaking at the service that day so you don't have to worry about walking out. Honey, I want you to know something. I can talk at Grandpa's funeral service because the Lord had me deal with the abuse a long time ago. It's been addressed and healed, and by God's grace it's been forgiven. That's why I can stand up and say what I'm going to say."

"Okay, Mom," she said hesitantly, "but if someone does start saying how wonderful he was, I'm out of there."

I prayed for several days about what would both honor my stepfather and honor God. This is what I shared that day:

Many of you who knew my dad well know he was a proud man. He was proud of:
- *Being a pilot and serving his country in World War II*
- *His athletic ability as a young man—being quarterback on his football team*
- *Being a "Hoosier" from the state of Indiana*
- *Being able to fix most any Singer sewing machine*
- *The many contributions made by the organizations he was a part of*
- *And although we didn't often hear it—he was proud of his children and grandchildren*

In most recent days, his proudest moments were his consecutive wins over my mom and others playing the game of Aggravation.

Honoring Dishonorable Parents

All of these were things he took pride in—however, what I value most is the legacy of faith that came through his influence in our family.

When my parents married in 1963, we began attending a Bible-believing church. That foundation has always been for me the treasure of my life. My dad came from a family in which honoring God was taught and lived. He brought to our family a heritage of faith, for which I am grateful.

Dad died Tuesday, January 17, forty one years ago to the day since I received Jesus Christ as my personal Savior.

I am a Christian today, not because dad lived a perfect life, but because of the grace of God and the power of Christ's redemptive work on the cross.

Dad is at peace and "all is settled in heaven."

There is no greater legacy to leave than this—a legacy of faith.

"For the things that are seen are temporary, but the things that are unseen are eternal."

Yes, my stepfather died January 17, 2006—on the forty-first anniversary of the day I asked Jesus into my life. When I received news of his death, I couldn't help but be in amazement and awe that the Lord would call my stepfather home on *that* day. I sensed the Spirit of God say to me, "All is settled in heaven." No doubt, the angels were rejoicing in heaven over another child of God who had finally come home.

We can honor even dishonorable parents because we rest in God's sovereignty and yield to His authority in our lives. It no longer is about what our parents have or have not done—it is about trusting God who loved us and gave His Son as a ransom for us.

There will always be authorities in our lives. Maturity entails learning to be subject to those in authority over us. James 4:7 tells us, "Submit yourselves, then, to God" (NIV). God designed the family to be the structure in which we learn how to do this. I realize now more than ever that the fifth commandment is essential to living a godly life. Honoring our parents is a lifelong process through which we are blessed. When we say "yes" to God's sovereignty and yield to His authority in our lives we can rest and be at peace in all that He allows, knowing that He is working to bring about His purposes for our good and His glory.

We have learned in this section the five essentials of honoring our parents in adulthood:

- Show *kindness* and *respect* for what they provided (1 Timothy 5:4)
- Speak *truth in love* when necessary (Ephesians 4:15)
- Set a *pattern of loving behavior* for your own children (1 Corinthians 11:1)
- Seek to *settle issues* as much as is possible (Romans 12:18)
- Submit to God's *authority* and *sovereignty* in your life (Psalm 139)

When we seek to honor our parents in these ways, we are honoring God. More often than not, I don't have within me the resources to carry out what I know God would have me do. That is when I cry out to God asking Him to impart to me what is so foreign to my fleshly nature and so much a part of His divine nature.

I have memorized and, on multiple occasions, preached the following verse to myself; may you clothe yourself with it today, empowered by His Spirit to honor your parents all the days of your life: "Therefore, as God's chosen people, holy and dearly loved, clothe yourselves with compassion, kindness, humility, gentleness and patience" (Colossians 3:12 NIV).

SECTION IV

THE BLESSINGS OF HONOR

Earlier when we looked at the Bible's teachings about honoring your father and your mother, I interviewed two Old Testament scholars, Dr. Sailhamer and Dr. Sunukjian. I thought it only fitting that I conclude the book with a brief interview with Jonathan Lunde, PhD, a New Testament scholar and professor at Talbot School of Theology of Biola University.[1] I asked Dr. Lunde specifically about how we are to understand the apostle Paul's admonition in Ephesians 6:1–3: "Children, obey your parents in the Lord, for this is right. 'Honor your father and mother'—which is the first commandment with a promise—'so that it may go well with you and that you may enjoy long life on the earth'" (NIV).

"I'm especially interested in that last verse," I told him. "How are we, in New Testament times, to understand the phrase 'that it may go well with you and that you may enjoy long life on the earth'?"

"Let me first ask you a question," said Dr. Lunde. "What is your understanding of the promise given in the Old Testament about the land? What do you understand the 'land' to represent?"

"I think that when God promised Israel that they would 'live long in the land,' the land represented the covenantal promise God originally made with Abraham and his descendants," I said rather tentatively.

"That is right," he said. He explained that in the Old Testament there are repeated references to the land as a covenantal blessing, and how the Israelites obedience to God's Law played an integral part in receiving that blessing.

"But, in the New Testament," Dr. Lunde added, "there is no mention of the land except as it is referred to in the coming kingdom. The 'land' in the New Testament disappears. It is really our covenantal relationship with God."

"I'm not sure I follow. Could you elaborate?" I asked.

"In the Old Testament, obedience to the covenant brought about blessing in the context of the land. Since in the New Testament there is no land per se, the blessings become spiritual ones."

"So are you saying that as we live faithfully in covenant with God today, we experience spiritual blessings rather than physical ones?" I asked.

"Not exactly. There is proverbial wisdom in following God's commands that may, in fact, suggest that we experience a healthier, lengthier life as Dr. Sunukjian suggested to you earlier. It is a pattern of living that leads to life," Dr. Lunde summarized.

I was beginning to understand. When Paul reiterated the fifth commandment in Ephesians, he was saying that the promise for those who obey their parents (or honor them once we become adults) is that we will enjoy a prosperous and long life on the earth. Many commentators agree that the general principle is that obedience/honor fosters self-discipline, which in turn brings stability and longevity to one's life.[2] But, Paul may also have been saying is that there are intrinsic spiritual blessings and benefits in our relationship with God when we honor our parents. The New Testament emphasizes in a new way those spiritual blessings, without completely setting aside the physical blessings described in the Old Testament.

As I reflected on this idea my life flashed in front of my eyes. I saw many significant markers along my own journey of learning what it meant to honor my parents. I thought about the intense longing I had for a father who loved me and how that longing drove me straight into the arms of my Abba Father as a young child.

I thought about many of the experiences I have chronicled in this book and how faithful God has been to walk me through the obstacles in my heart and show me His way. I couldn't help but think of the verse in Psalm 27:10 as paraphrased in *The Message*: "My father and mother walked out and left me, but GOD took me in."

There have been countless blessings that have come to my life through this journey. Above all, I have felt God's presence and power and experienced His deep love for me as we have walked the road together. For years I prayed that I would know the love of God so deeply that nothing could shake me. I haven't arrived there yet, but I'm further along the journey because of His grace.

There are myriad blessings that I could highlight as I reflect upon my journey of honoring my parents, however, there are four distinct ones that we will look at in the next section: the blessing of relinquishment, the blessing of peace, the blessing of giving grace and the blessing of obedience.

Chapter 14

THE BLESSING OF RELINQUISHMENT

"I can't believe our paths crossed today!" Linda said. "I have to share with you what just happened."

Linda was a former client who had sought counseling for help in dealing with her mother.

"My mother just passed away and the memorial service was yesterday," Linda said peacefully.

"How are you feeling? Did everything go alright?" I asked.

"It went very well. I was even able to speak at her service," Linda said smiling. "Jan, it wouldn't have been possible without the work we did. I was able to share some things at her service that were meaningful to me and I'm so thankful to God for the way He's allowed me to heal and let go."

Years before, Linda had been in charge of her mother's care. She and her mother had always had a difficult relationship due to her mother's critical nature. Nothing she did was ever good enough in her mother's eyes.

In the course of treatment, it became clear to Linda that she needed to relinquish the care of her mother to her brother. She told her brother that she would be limiting contact with her mother for a period of time in order to heal. This period lasted about four years.

Linda made progress in her own growth and began to see her mother as a troubled woman whose own background contributed to her inability to love and nurture her children. She educated herself about her mother's mental condition, gaining insight into why her mother acted and reacted the way she did.

Linda came to understand that she had spent her entire life trying to "please" her mother and win her approval. She realized her mother had become an "idol" in her life; she was focusing on performing, sacrificing, and giving to her, in order to be loved. Linda grieved the loss of the mother she wished she had and began to accept the one she'd been given. She came to understand how much God wanted to fill those empty places in her life with His love and the love of other people around her.

I could see the tranquility on her face as she shared these things with me. She had made peace with her mother long before her mother stepped into eternity.

Linda smiled and said, "Jan, that separation was not only beneficial to me, it also helped my mother find new ways to relate to other people. I'm so grateful for all that God did. I let her go emotionally a long time ago and that enabled me to say goodbye yesterday with no regrets."

In their book, *The Mom Factor,* Henry Cloud and John Townsend write:

> Mom was probably not a villain. She most likely did not reject your real self just because she felt like it. She was probably under her own ideal self demands from her own mother or someone else who was significant to her. She continued those negative patterns in her interactions with you, placing the same demands

on you that she labored under herself. To remember and try to understand mom's frailties and accept them is to begin to love her as she is.[1]

Honoring sometimes means *relinquishment*. Relinquishment may take many different forms, but it always includes forgiveness. I don't know that any of us can genuinely honor our parents without going through the process of forgiving them.[2] Yes, you may act in external ways that are honorable toward them, but unless you deal with the issues of your heart it is only halfhearted honor.

You've probably heard a number of sermons about forgiveness and about forgiving from the heart. (Matthew 18:35 NIV) The Greek word translated "forgiveness" in our Bibles literally means "to send away, let go, give up a debt."[3] When Scripture talks about the heart, we often think of it only as our emotions; however, in the Bible the heart is both the "rational and emotional elements of a man's being."[4]

So, when we forgive there is both a rational side and an emotional side. All too often, I encounter people who have given mental assent to forgiving their parents and acted honorably toward them, but they've neglected to do the painful work of the emotional side. I'm not saying that one should avoid acting honorably toward their parents until such time as their heart is in agreement with their head, but I am saying that it is important that the process be completed. Otherwise we will resemble the Pharisees whom Jesus indicted for honoring God with their lips, while their hearts remained far from him. Throughout Scripture, God is always most concerned about our hearts, not just our behavior.

In their book, *Forgiving Our Parents Forgiving Ourselves,* Stoop and Masteller write: "Forgiveness as a decision means choosing not to hold onto an emotional 'debt' against another person. Forgiveness as a process means working through our own inner reactions until what was done to us no longer dominates us."[5] They further state that "the process of forgiveness is complete when what happened between us is no longer a 'live issue' in the way I think of you and relate to you, or in the way I live my life."[6]

This was clearly illustrated for us in Linda's life and relationship with her mother.

For some of us relinquishment may also include giving up wishes and ideal expectations in relationship to our parents.

Unfulfilled Hopes

Several years ago, I had a conversation with my biological father that wounded me deeply. My dad asked my opinion about a situation with my niece, my oldest sister's adult daughter. When I didn't readily offer an opinion, he persisted. I finally said, "Dad, it really doesn't matter what I think. This is an issue between Sheryl and her daughter. It's not really up to me to say what should happen for them."

"Well, you're probably right. You're not *really* my daughter anyway," he said in a matter-of-fact tone.

I could hardly believe what I was hearing. I asked, "What do you mean by that?'

"Well, legally you aren't my daughter—you were adopted, so you're not really my daughter anymore." I managed not to lash back, but through tears I said, "That really hurts me. Why are you saying that to me?" He said rather coldly, "Because it's true—you're not really my daughter."

I hung up the phone shortly thereafter, devastated. I couldn't believe my dad "disowned" me. I immediately ran to my husband and recounted the conversation. My husband Don was very dear. He took me in his arms and said, "Oh, honey, that is awful. I can't believe a dad would ever say such a thing to his own flesh and blood. I'm so sorry that happened." He held me for a long time and I wept. The reality of never having a dad who genuinely loved me cut me to the core.

I sensed finality in that moment. In order to safeguard my heart,

I decided to limit contact with my biological father. I phoned once a month as a gesture of honor and kept the conversation short and pleasant, but I would not engage my heart.

A little history may help here. After my parents' divorce when I was five there was little contact with my father. He was sporadic in his visits and his child support. As children we were not allowed to speak of my father and on the few occasions when he did take us for visitation, the emotional cost of being with him was too much.

My middle sister moved out abruptly at eighteen and sought refuge with my father. The unspoken issues at home intensified. My stepfather sought to adopt me legally at age fourteen. I felt pressured by my parents to write a letter to my father and the court saying that I was in favor of being adopted. No one ever asked about any abuse, so the adoption was approved and my father relinquished his parental rights. My father never forgave me for that letter. It had to be so hurtful for him to read that his fourteen-year-old daughter no longer wanted him to be her father.

When I turned eighteen, I decided to reestablish contact with my father at the encouragement of my Christian boss.

I didn't realize for many years that there was still a little girl inside me that longed to have a daddy who loved her. I found myself pursuing a relationship with my father to my own detriment. Even as an adult married woman I kept hoping my dad would step into my life and want to know me and have a relationship with me. I was disappointed time after time. It took me several years to realize that my biological father was himself ill-equipped to form any meaningful relationships. For years I felt such personal rejection it was difficult for me not to be deeply hurt. Although I prayerfully asked God on numerous occasions to help me forgive my dad, there was not an immediate answer. Instead God was working at an even deeper level in my heart to make my heart fully yielded to Him . . . and from there, prompt forgiveness.

Gradually Letting Go

In the spring of 2008 while speaking at a women's retreat, I received an urgent call from my husband. My sister who lived near my father had just rushed him to the emergency room and he was in serious condition. I prayed and asked the Lord what I was to do. Was I to leave the retreat and go to the hospital? Was my father going to die? Had I done everything God had asked of me with regard to him?

I heard the Lord say clearly to me, "Release him completely." As I worked through different emotions of sadness, disappointment, anger, and rejection, I realized God was asking me to let my father go. I sensed that God was saying to release him from all the expectations that I had of him and to release the anger and resentment that had built up over the years. This was not easy, but to the best of my ability I attempted to do so.

As it turned out, my father recovered to celebrate his ninetieth birthday a year later.

Milestone or Millstone

"Hi Dad, it's Jan," I said. "You've got a big birthday coming up. This is quite a milestone."

"Yep, I never thought I'd make it," said my soon to be ninety-year-old biological father.

"We got the invitation from Sheryl, and Don and I will be coming to your birthday celebration," I said positively.

"Why are you coming?" he replied curtly. "You didn't come to my eightieth birthday." I remained silent for a few seconds and then said, "This is quite a milestone birthday and we'd like to come and celebrate it with you."

Again, my father retorted, "I don't know why you're coming. You know your sister Karen isn't coming. She's still mad about our money conversation. You don't have to come either. You missed the last birthday, so I don't know why you're coming." I chose to remain silent again, this time for a few more seconds. Then my father said, "Is there something wrong with your phone? I don't hear you responding."

I breathed a quick prayer and said, "Dad, Don and I are planning to be at your birthday party to celebrate this milestone with you. Would you prefer that we not come?"

"No, I'm glad you're coming, it should be a nice party," he said with a chuckle.

"Good," I said, "we're glad to be coming too. So, I'll see you next week."

I hung up the phone shaking my head. This was so typical of our conversations. You may be wondering why I kept coming back for more. I have to be honest: I've wondered about that myself. Over the years I have prayed for my dad's salvation and have spoken with him numerous times about what it means to be a Christian. I think in some way I felt a measure of responsibility for his salvation. I thought that if I just loved him enough he would be open to the truth of the gospel. This was a heavy load to carry, but God gradually released me from my self-imposed burden.

I also thought for years that I was under obligation to honor him, even though he did not raise me. It wasn't until my conversation with Dr. Sunukjian that I learned differently. I also didn't realize that my persistent pursuit of relationship was really spawned by the little girl inside of me who was still desperately seeking her daddy's love. There was a new level of grief and sadness that had to be faced before I could genuinely let go. "We cannot let go of mother [or father] if we are still needing something from her [or him.]"[7]

We went to his birthday celebration at my sister's home and it was a lovely evening of tribute to my father. Somehow, even before attending his party, I sensed the Lord was releasing me from my monthly obligation to phone my father. It seemed like God was saying I had done my part in honoring him over the years and that it was not my responsibility to maintain a connection. I felt released from making regular contact, but it wasn't out of anger or defeatism—it was simply the outward expression of letting go.

Release through Gratitude

I was prompted to write a letter to my dad several months after his birthday celebration. I remembered hearing Dennis Rainey's radio program about writing your parents a tribute while they are still living.[8] At first, I didn't know if there was anything I could say. I prayed about it for several days. Finally, I sat down to write what would prove not only to be the closure that I needed but also a way to honor my father genuinely while he still lived. Here is what I wrote:

Dearest Dad,

You have been on my mind lately. I have some things I want to share with you, but I wanted to write them in a letter rather than speak with you by phone. I wanted you to hear these words from me before you die or are in a state where you are not able to really take them in.

I have been reflecting about my life and family and I realized that I have never let you know some things that I have appreciated about you. I don't have a lot of memories with you in my childhood since the divorce occurred when I was so young. But I do have three very special memories that warm my heart when I think of them.

I remember one Halloween, when we lived on Fremontia in San Bernardino, that you sat at a card table and passed out candy to all the children who came to our door. This somehow made me feel good as a little girl that my dad would greet other little children and give them candy.

Another memory was in that same house. I remember you, Sid, and mom sitting in the kitchen at our table, talking and laughing together. I have no idea what was being said, but I remember the laughter.

Finally, the most precious memory I have was when I was five and was in St. Bernardine's hospital having my tonsils removed. It was dark and late at night and I was crying in my hospital bed because I was afraid and alone. I remember looking out the window and I saw you. You came to visit me and it felt like God had answered the prayer of a tiny little girl who needed her daddy.

Through the years, our relationship has not always been as close as I would have wished, but I want you to know that I am grateful to God for you, as my father. God certainly knew the events in my life and how He would weave things together in a way that would make me the woman that I am today. He chose to use some of the most difficult circumstances to bring about His purposes and you have played a most significant role toward those ends.

I especially want to thank you for several things. You've always remembered to acknowledge my birthday through a card or phone call, and I appreciate that a lot. You made time to visit our home on several occasions and to stay with us a few times too, which was very meaningful to me and my family. You shared in my girls' graduations and in Heather's wedding, and that was special. One of my fondest memories as an adult is the time we visited you at your condo in San Diego. You got your guitar out of the closet and played and sang for us. It was a sweet time for us as a family and especially for Heather because of her musical interests.

I know I have thanked you before, but I want you to know how deeply grateful I am to you for paying for my Master's Degree. That was a very kind thing for you to do as it allowed me to proceed down a path toward my career and ministry that I have dearly loved. You didn't have to contribute to my education, but you did. In that way, God has used you in my ministry to thousands of people all over the world through my speaking and my books. Thank you so much, Dad!

We had a conversation last year and we talked about faith. I asked you what you believed about Jesus and you said that you knew that He died on the cross for your sins. When I asked you if you knew if you'd go to heaven when you died, you acknowledged that you would, not on the basis of anything you had done, but on the basis of accepting Jesus and His sacrifice of dying for your sins. I told you that was all I needed to hear because I wanted you to be in heaven and it's only on the basis of what Jesus did for us that we are forgiven. We can't earn heaven by our good works or by being good people. We are loved and forgiven and it is only by the gift of God's grace that we are saved.

In the past, you expressed regret over the divorce but I want you to know that I forgive you and release you from any guilt that you may still hold in your heart. God has an amazing ability to redeem our mistakes and failures and use those very things to bring about good in our lives and glory to Him. I also want you to know that you don't owe me anything. I have been blessed beyond what I could ever imagine or deserve. I have been the recipient of God's grace in such abundance that it is difficult for me to put it into words.

Finally, I just want to say that I love you and thank God for you. He has used you in ways that you will never completely know or understand in this life. I hope this letter finds you well and that you will take to heart all that I've shared. Thank you, Dad, for everything.

May God's blessings and joy be yours!
With love and gratitude,
Jan

Sometimes, honoring our parents means letting go and releasing them from the needs and expectations that were never met in childhood and cannot be met by them in adulthood. At some point in time, honoring our parents means that we accept what will never be and learn to live in gratitude for what is. It means that we honor our parents for the position they were given in God's sovereignty and we shift our focus and our needs to the only One who is able to fill our deepest longings.

God continues to do a deeper work of healing in my heart. Through this time, I have discovered things about my own intense longings for my father's love and approval that were misplaced. Whether he could not or would not meet them is not the issue. These longings were mine and they came from a little girl whose heart could not be healed by her earthly father—only by her Heavenly Father.

God's Gracious Gift

Recently, I had a new insight. I thought that God preserved my father's life so as to give him more opportunities to come to know him as his Savior. What became clear to me for the first time was this: God preserved my father's life not only for him, but also for me. My Abba Father has graciously given me time so that I might have peace with my dad before he dies. It is the final release that I needed. It's the acceptance that God did not make a mistake. He chose from the foundations of the world that I would be born of my father, that I would carry within me part of his DNA, that I would suffer the abandonment and loss of my parents divorce—but he had also ordained that through it all I would see my need for a Savior. I know that is why I came to faith as a young child at the age of ten. It was my deep longing for my father that drew me to my Abba Father—God in his graciousness uses our deepest heartaches to bring about redemption. It is the story of my life.

You may be at the point of relinquishment, realizing it is time to let go. You, like me, may have longed for years to have a relationship with a parent that has proved futile.⁹ Your every attempt to make the relationship work has left you devastated. As much as you have told yourself that you're a grown person who should be able to move on without needing your parents' love and approval, you recognize there is still a void inside. God understands. He made each of us with a deep need for attachment to our parents; when that attachment has been broken or never realized we feel empty. If that is true of you, you may need to find people with whom you can connect and share your feelings of loss and disappointment. Grieving through our losses and disappointments should never be done in isolation.

I learned a very important principle early in my own recovery process; when we've been sinned against relationally, God uses reparative relationships to heal us. It happens as we enter deeply into relationship with God and with other people who can be trusted to walk alongside us in our journey. We learn to relinquish what will never be in order to receive what was meant to be—an intimate relationship with our Abba Father whose unconditional love and mercy never fails, whose grace is sufficient, and whose blessings are unlimited.

> *The quality of mercy is not strained.*
> *It droppeth as the gentle rain from heaven*
> *Upon the place beneath. It is twice blest:*
> *It blesseth him that gives and him that takes.*¹⁰

Chapter 15

THE BLESSING OF PEACE

It wasn't long after the closure with my biological father that I had a conversation with my mom that was a surprise blessing. It came by way of Oprah.

Early in our conversation, my mom revealed that she was upset about something.

"What's wrong, Mom?" I asked

"Did you happen to see Oprah today?"

"No, Mom, why do you ask?"

"I wish you would have watched it today. It was very upsetting," she said in a troubled tone. She went on to describe the story related by Oprah's guest that day. He'd experienced severe physical and emotional abuse as a child from his mother and from several of her boyfriends. Now a married adult, he struggled with nightmares and had difficulty relating to his wife sexually.

The last time my mom brought up something about abuse in her community I'd said nothing. I'd hung up the phone, bewildered that she could talk with me about the subject with little connection or compassion for me. I'd told a therapist friend about the conversation and she commented that maybe that had been the closest my mom could come to acknowledging how wrong my stepfather's actions had been. That made a lot of sense to me. But it still left a part of me feeling sad. My mother never wanted to hear about my pain. She never asked about what I'd experienced.

Now, here we were again, my mom broaching this sensitive subject apparently unconcerned about my own painful past. I breathed a prayer and then said, "Mom, you know it's kind of hard for me to hear you talk about this. You seem to have more compassion for this man on TV than you've ever shown to me."

"Well, you weren't beat up every day like he was," she said somewhat dismissively.

"No, Mom, I wasn't. But I did struggle with intimacy with my husband in our early years of marriage and I've spent thousands of dollars on therapy."

"Well, as I watched this show I kept thinking about your dad. You know, he was abused by his grandmother. Just watching this man tell his story stirred up a lot of things. He was only seven years old when these things began. He's had to deal with a lot of things and it took a huge toll in his life."

"Mom, I was seven years old when it started with Dad. What is hard for me is that you've never really asked or wanted to know what happened. You know that I've forgiven Dad and by God's grace my heart has healed. I'm not trying to make you feel guilty. I just want you to understand how your compassion for the man on TV causes me to wish you had some for me."

"I know I was a bad mother. I should have protected you girls," she said with conviction.

"Mom, we all mess up as parents. Remember last week when I told you about the letter I wrote to Heather? I had to admit some of my mistakes too."

"We all do the best we can," she said.

"Mom, the most important thing is that we can talk about it. We can't change the past, but one of the best gifts we give our children is taking responsibility for our actions and showing them compassion. I know this conversation is hard for you, but you've given me a gift today. I'm so glad we were able to talk a little about this. It means a lot to hear you say you wish you had protected us. One of the hardest things about the abuse by Dad was going through it all alone with no one to help me. God has been so faithful and has healed that little girl's heart—and I'm grateful we could talk today."

That was the extent of the conversation, but it was a blessing. That was the first time in my life that my mom ever said anything about wishing she'd protected me. It was also the first time she'd ever been emotionally present for me. I know it has been painfully lonely for my mom since my stepfather's death. I'm grateful to God that I have had these years to establish a deeper connection with her which has been marked by peacefulness. We have navigated through some troubled waters over the years; the writing of my first book, *Door of Hope*, which detailed my journey through the recovery process from sexual abuse; the boundaries my husband and I established for the protection of our daughters; the disclosure of the abuse to my half brother. So many issues arose over the years for which I needed God's wisdom, direction, and grace. There is always the delicate balance of honoring my parents, and yet, being obedient to the call on my life to write and speak of God's redemptive work in my heart and our family.

I know there have been some over the years who've wondered if talking about such things has any value or any place within the Christian community. What I have learned over the last thirty years of ministry is that God wastes nothing. When I recommitted my life to Him when I was twenty two I said, "Lord, if you can do anything with the mess I've made, I give you my life." It's our life surrendered to Him that He uses—

not just our cleaned up version, not just our strengths, not just the stellar moments of success or fame, not just the times we got it right with our own children, but *all* of who we are.

We've talked about the blessing of relinquishment and the blessing of peace that comes from an authentic honoring of our parents. We're going to see in the next chapter a double blessing.

Chapter 16

THE BLESSING OF GIVING GRACE

Several years ago the Spirit of God prompted me to invite my stepfather out to lunch for Father's Day. I was totally caught off guard. Although it had been over fifteen years since the initial confrontation regarding the abuse and we had restored a loving relationship, I never had the occasion to be with my stepfather alone. I struggled in prayer asking the Lord why *I* was always the one extending love to my stepfather when *he* was the one who ravaged my life. I told the Lord I didn't think I could do it. *How can we sit across the table from each other and carry on a meaningful conversation? What will we talk about?* I felt ashamed for feeling this way and began questioning the forgiveness I believed God had worked in my heart.

I cried most of the way up to my parents' home and on the way asked the Lord again why He wanted me to do this. I heard Him say very clearly, *I have a blessing in it for you*. I thought to myself, *I could use a blessing*, and continued the drive, wondering what that blessing might be.

As my stepfather and I sat across from each other at lunch, we talked about my step-grandfather and his godly influence and character. We laughed and reminisced about family vacations and my grandpa Ray. In the back of my mind I thought the "blessing" God had in store for me was something my stepfather might say to affirm me in some way. Affirmation was something that was scarce around my home growing up.

I was wrong. I was totally unprepared for the blessing God had for me. Toward the end of our lunch, my stepfather looked across the table at me with tears running down his cheeks and said, "Jan, thank you so much for taking me out to lunch today—you don't know how much this has meant to me." Just then, a rush of compassion and grace flooded my heart. As I looked at my stepfather, I didn't see the man that had abused me for eleven years. I saw a man in desperate need of the grace and mercy of a Savior who died for us all. The blessing was clear. In that moment, God infused *me* with that grace, mercy, and love for *him*, afresh again.

I looked at my stepfather with tears in my own eyes and said, "Dad, you are *so* welcome."

As I drove home, the Lord reminded me that one of the greatest blessings is *giving grace to one who is undeserving.* I looked at myself in my rearview mirror and thanked Him all the way home for *His* grace, mercy, and love in my life.[1]

Chapter 17

THE BLESSINGS OF OBEDIENCE

I have a confession to make. I felt God calling me to write this book for four years before I said "yes."

I could not imagine tackling such a topic, nor did I feel qualified to address the meaning of what honoring parents looks like today in our world. Finally, one spring while teaching the book of James in my women's Bible study, my disobedience was no longer tolerable. I announced to the audience of one hundred women that I could not stand before them teaching concepts like "Be a doer of the word and not a hearer only" with any integrity when I myself was failing to obey what I knew God was calling me to do. As a result, I asked them to pray for me and I took the following year off from teaching to dedicate myself to the writing.

Although I felt inadequate in so many areas, I was burdened for the many who crossed my path weekly who seemed to be struggling with these issues: whether it was the young mom in my Bible study whose mother-in-law was meddling, the thirty-six year-old man whose father was an alcoholic, or the sixty-three-year-old man who was caring both for his aging mother and his wife who had breast cancer. I empathized with the anguish I saw on each of their faces; they desperately wanted to do what was right in God's eyes. But they often struggled not only with what honor might look like in their particular situation, but also with the convoluted emotions that surfaced in dealing with their parents.

My desire in writing has always been to encourage people who find themselves in need of hope. That's not to say that I think I have a corner on what it means to honor our parents. As evidenced in this book, I have wrestled through these issues on many different levels, earnestly seeking to follow God's command. As a result, I've experienced God's blessing along the way—but not because I did everything perfectly. God's grace has covered me, corrected me, and consoled me throughout this journey. I can never thank Him enough for His faithfulness.

In the beginning of the book, I talked about how the fifth commandment is a *commandment for life*. It is a commandment that we are to observe for our entire lifetime and it is a commandment that promises to provide a foundational stability for our life when followed. As we stand before God on that final day, we will stand alone. No one else will have the opportunity to provide input, opinions, justifications, or rationalizations. It's just me before God and He will determine whether or not I have been obedient to Him by honoring my parents.

Before we look at what honor might look in your life, let me share how obedience to this command has been a life transforming process in my life. There are three distinct blessings that have borne fruit in my life because of this journey of obedience: freedom from the past; joy; and gratitude.

As I reflect upon my journey, I realize that step by step, day by day, and year by year, God was faithfully birthing more and more freedom into my life. That freedom has inherently been woven through extending forgiveness to my parents, who themselves were bound up by hurts, unmet needs from their childhoods, and sinful choices. I've discovered that

I am not only experiencing freedom *from* the past, but also, I am freer in the present to be who God created me. What an unexpected gift!

I've been surprised by the joy that has flooded my heart as God has allowed me to be a conduit of His love and mercy to my frail, aging, and emotionally fragile parents. I found that in the early days of my journey there seemed to be more angst and unyielding bitterness, but these days are characterized by much more kindness, gentleness, and patience.

And finally, gratitude has burgeoned forth as I've learned to rest more fully in my Father God's love and sovereignty. I find that my prayers are more filled with thanksgiving and praise than ever before. I've found the freedom, joy, and gratitude that could only come through walking this journey in companionship with Jesus, the Lover of my soul and the One who paid the ultimate price for me.

My prayer for you, beloved reader, is that somehow by God's grace my own journey and the journeys of others detailed in this book has offered you some practical help in navigating through your own situation, but more importantly, that it's given you hope.

AN INVITATION: HONOR IN YOUR LIFE

I wonder, what honoring your parents might look like in your life? Maybe you've grown up in a loving Christian home, but you've never taken the time to tell your parents how grateful you are for all that they've cemented into your life. For others of you, honoring poses a challenge. You may have parents who are alcoholics or parents who are antagonistic toward your faith. Some of you might have parents who abused or abandoned you. Still others of you might have parents whose habitual patterns have caused you emotional suffering that is not easily remedied.

I wonder if you'd be willing to ask the Lord how you might begin to honor your parents in light of what is true—*remembering what honor is and what it is not*. Some of you may need to review specific chapters in this book to help you integrate the meaning of *respect and responsiveness* as you interface with your parents, keeping in mind the model Jesus gave us. Some of you might need to obtain some professional help in grieving through the losses of your childhood so that you can get to the place of forgiveness and relinquishment.

Others of you might benefit from joining a support group to help you discern whether your involvement with your parents has become entwined with some unhealthy family patterns. Some of you may need to review on a regular basis the five fundamentals of living out honor as adults.

Over the years, I've certainly grown in my understanding of what it means to "honor dishonorable parents." By God's grace, I'm still learning what honor means, what it doesn't mean, and how to live it out in adulthood in a God-honoring way.

My prayer is that God will lead you in the path of honor that is right for you. No matter where that path may lead, I can assure you of one thing: *when you honor your parents, you honor God—and in doing so, you receive the blessing.*

> "Honor your father and your mother, as the Lord your God
> has commanded you, so that you may live long and that it may
> go well with you in the land the Lord your God is giving you."
> (Deuteronomy 5:16 NIV)

EPILOGUE

In early July 2012, my mother's cancer returned and she had to resume chemotherapy. Her oncologist was hopeful since she had been cancer free for nearly five years.

My husband and I were scheduled to leave on vacation in the latter part of July, so I promised to spend one day a week helping my mom around her home prior to our leaving. She was a bit tired due to the aftereffects of her treatment, but she was in good spirits. We laughed, shared stories, and just enjoyed the uninterrupted time together. Just before saying goodbye on that final visit before our vacation, I bent over to kiss her and, taking both of her hands in mine, said, "Mom, I love you so much—and I'm so grateful to the Lord for these last six years. It's felt like I got my mama back." We looked into each other's tear-filled eyes and said our goodbye, not realizing it would be our last.

Toward the end of our vacation, my brother called to say my mom had been admitted to the hospital for what seemed to be an infection. He assured me that it wasn't an emergency and he would keep me informed. Within two days, what we thought was an infection went systemic but the doctors remained optimistic.[1] Our scheduled flight was a red-eye so I arrived early on a Friday morning and drove immediately to the hospital.

My brother met me at the entrance to my mother's room saying she'd been incoherent for over a day and didn't seem to recognize anyone. When we entered her room, my brother announced in a loud voice, "Mom, Jan's here." But there was no response. I walked over to the side of her bed, bent down and whispered in her ear, "Mama, it's Jan. I'm here now." Her eyes flickered open for a millisecond and she smiled.

Over the rest of that day, I sat with her, prayed, sang old hymns, and read Scripture to her. Her breathing was labored and she remained unresponsive. My brother and I got a call from the hospital early the next morning. Her vital signs were decreasing.

Shortly after we arrived, the attending physician came in the room and asked if there was anything else we needed and verified my mother's wishes of "no heroics." He asked us how old our mother was and if she'd had a good life. We answered, "Eighty three, and yes, she's had a good life." He then said reassuringly, "Well, that's good. This is the way it should be, with her children by her side, going peacefully." We couldn't have agreed more.

Shortly afterward, mom's breathing became very labored and both my brother and I reassured her that she could "leave us." After several minutes I looked up at my younger brother and asked if he wanted me to pray that "Jesus would take her." He said a simple "yes." I bowed and began to pray and then I whispered in my mom's ear, "Mama, it's okay. You can let go. Jesus is waiting for you at the gate. He's waiting to welcome His daughter home." A few minutes went by and we saw my mom take her last breath and a sweet peace pervaded the room. My brother and I cried in each other's arms.

A few days later, my brother phoned as we were planning mom's service, and said how glad he was that it was just the two of us with her at the end. Then he said something I will never forget. "I have to tell you, that experience was one of the most beautiful experiences of my life." *Mine too*, I thought to myself.

The same Sovereign God who ushered me into this world and placed me in a home with my chosen parents granted me the gracious privilege of walking alongside my mom to the very moment He ushered her from this life into His eternal presence. May His name be forever praised!

> "'He will wipe every tear from their eyes. There will be no more death' or mourning or crying or pain, for the old order of things has passed away." He who was seated on the throne said, "I am making everything new!"
> (Revelation 21:4–5 NIV)

ENDNOTES

Chapter 1:

1. Harold H. Bloomfield, M.D. with Leonard Felder, Ph.D., *Making Peace with Your Parents: The Key to Enriching Your Life and All Your Relationships* (New York: Ballantine Books,1983), 56
2. Bloomfield, *Making Peace with Your Parents*, 53

Chapter 2:

1. Jan Frank, *Door of Hope: Recognizing and Resolving the Pains of Your Past* (Nashville, TN: Thomas Nelson Publishers, 1995),189
2. Charles Sell, *Unfinished Business: Helping Adult Children Resolve Their Past* (Portland, OR; Multnomah,1989), 42
3. Rich Buhler, *Pain and Pretending: You Can Be Set Free from the Hurts of the Past* (Nashville, TN: Thomas Nelson Publishers,1988), 103
4. Randy Alcorn, *The Grace and Truth Paradox: Responding with Christlike Balance* (Portland, OR: Multnomah, 2009), 88

Chapter 3:

1. Merriam-Webster, Incorporated, *MerriamWebster's Collegiate Dictionary*, Tenth Edition (Springfield, Massachusetts: Merriam Webster, 1994), 530

2. Dr. Susan Forward with Craig Buck, *Toxic Parents: Overcoming Their Hurtful Legacy and Reclaiming Your Life* (New York: Bantam Books, 1989), 7
3. Forward, *Toxic Parents*, 6
4. Ibid, 5
5. Dr. Henry Cloud & Dr. John Townsend, *Boundaries: When To Say Yes How to Say No To Take Control of Your Life* (Grand Rapids, MI: Zondervan, 1992), 38
6. David Stoop, Ph.D., *Forgiving the Unforgivable* (Ventura, CA: Regal, 2005), 104

Chapter 4:

1. Howard M. Halpern, Ph.D., *Cutting Loose: An Adult's Guide to Coming to Terms with Your Parents* (New York: Simon & Schuster Inc., 1990), 13-14

Chapter 5:

1. Alcohol Self-Help News http://alcoholselfhelpnews.wordpress.com/
2. Darrell L. Bock, Th.M., Ph.D., editor, *The Bible Knowledge Word Study, Acts-Ephesians* (Colorado Springs; Cook Communications Ministries, 2006), 412
3. Bock, *The Bible Knowledge Word Study*, 413

Chapter 6:

1. Dr. Henry Cloud & Dr. John Townsend, *Boundaries: When to Say Yes How to Say No To Take Control of Your Life* (Grand Rapids, MI: Zondervan, 1992), 86
2. Dr. Donald R. Sunukjian, in discussion with the author, November 9, 2009
3. Mark Sichel, CSW, *Healing from Family Rifts: Ten Steps to Finding Peace After Being Cut Off From a Family Member* (New York: McGraw-Hill, 2004), 81
4. Dr. Henry Cloud & Dr. John Townsend, *The Mom Factor* (Grand Rapids, MI: Zondervan, 1996), 178

Chapter 7:

1. Dr. John Sailhamer, in discussion with the author, July 19, 2010
2. Dr. Donald R. Sunukjian, in discussion with the author, November 9, 2009
3. James Strong, LL.D. S.T.D., *The New Strong's Expanded Dictionary of Bible Words*, (Nashville, TN: Thomas Nelson Publishers, 2001), 1412
4. Matthew 15:4,19:19; Mark 7:10, 10:19; Luke 18:20
5. Matthew 15:6 and Mark 7:11

Chapter 8:

1. Mark 6:3 lists the names of Jesus' half-brothers and mentions at least two unnamed half-sisters. These are the children born to Joseph and Mary after Jesus' birth. John F. Walvoord & Roy B. Zuck, eds, *The Bible Knowledge Commentary NT: An Exposition of the Scriptures by Dallas Seminary Faculty* (Colorado Spring, CO, 1983), 126-7
2. John 7: 3-9 discusses Jesus' relationship with his brothers. Since my focus is specifically on Jesus and His parents, I have not included this passage in our discussion.
3. Darrell L. Bock, *The NIV Application Commentary: Luke* (Grand Rapids, MI: Zondervan, 1996), 100
4. Ibid, 100
5. James Strong, *The New Strong's Expanded Dictionary of Bible Words* (Nashville: TN: Thomas Nelson Publishers, 2001), 1260-61 citation: *3600-01*, Greek word pronounced "od-oo-nah-o)
6. Strong's Bible Dictionary, 1432
7. Herbert Lockyer, *All the Women of the Bible* (Grand Rapids, MI: Zondervan), 97
8. Walvoord & Zuck, *Bible Knowledge Commentary NT*, 278
9. Ibid, 278
10. Lockyer, *All the Women of the Bible*, 97
11. As an adult, Jesus made His home in Capernaum with occasional stays in Bethany at the home of Martha, Mary, and Lazarus. Walvoord & Zuck, *The Bible Knowledge Commentary NT*, 215; Lockyer, All *The Women of the Bible*, 87

12. Walvoord & Zuck, *The Bible Knowledge Commentary NT*, 115
13. Ibid
14. Ibid
15. Spiros Zodhiates, Th. D, ed., *The Complete Word Study Dictionary NT* (Chatanooga, TN: AMG Publishers, 1992), 885
16. Michael J. Wilkins, *The NIV Application Commentary: Matthew*, (Grand Rapids, MI: Zondervan 2009), 454
17. Walvoord & Zuck, *The Bible Knowledge Commentary NT*, 118
18. John's account of the events at the cross is less descriptive than the account in the other gospels. For further detail it may be helpful to read Matthew 27:27-55, Mark 15:21-41, and Luke 23:26-49
19. Walvoord & Zuck, *The Bible Knowledge Commentary NT*, 188
20. D.A. Carson, *The Gospel According to John* (Grand Rapids, MI: William B. Eerdmans Publishing Company, 1991) , 617 (See also Mark 15:40 and Matthew 27: 55-56)
21. Lockyer, *All the Women of the Bible*, 98
22. Walvoord & Zuck, *The Bible Knowledge Commentary NT*, 340
23. Donald Davidson, *It Happened to Them* (as quoted in *All the Women of the Bible*, Lockyer, 99)

Chapter 9:

1. Dr. Henry Cloud & Dr. John Townsend, *The Mom Factor* (Grand Rapids, MI: Zondervan, 1996), 153

Chapter 10:

1. Howard M. Halpern, Ph. D., *Cutting Loose: An Adult's Guide to Coming to Terms with Your Parents* (New York: Simon & Schuster Inc., 1990), 21
2. "Being Brook" by Jenny Allen, Good Housekeeping January 2010; CMG08345 Vol.250 No.1; p.119

Chapter 11:

1. Dr. Henry Cloud & Dr. John Townsend, *How People Grow: What the Bible Reveals About Personal Growth* (Grand Rapids, MI: Zondervan, 2001), 140
2. "The Profound Power of a Legacy" FamilyLife Today, [radio broadcast transcript] (Los Angeles, CA KKLA, October 7, 2010)

Chapter 12:

1. James Strong, LL. D., S.T.D., *Strong's Expanded Dictionary of Bible Words* (Nashville, TN: Thomas Nelson Publishers, 2001), 1062
2. Douglas J. Moo, *The Life Application Bible Commentary: Romans* (Grand Rapids, MI: 2000), 242
3. Merriam-Webster, Incorporated, *MerriamWebster's Collegiate Dictionary*, Tenth Edition (Springfield, Massachusetts: Merriam Webster, 1994), 977
4. David Stoop, Ph.D., *Forgiving the Unforgivable* (Ventura, CA: Regal, 2005), 48
5. Acts 23:16 is the only reference we have of Paul's family reaction to his ministry. His nephew (his sister's son) is privy to a Jewish plot to kill Paul as he's being transported to Caesarea. His nephew informs Paul, and the centurion commander in charge of his transport, and the plot is foiled.
6. Beth Moore, *To Live is Christ* (Nashville, TN: B & H Publishing Group, 2001), 58
7. Clinton E. Arnold, general editor, *Zondervan Illustrated Bible Backgrounds Commentary: Acts* (Grand Rapids, MI: 2002), 80,82
8. Charles Sell, *Unfinished Business: Helping Adult Children Resolve Their Past* (Portland, OR: Multnomah Press, 1989), 41-42

Chapter 13:

1. Townsend, John, *Boundaries with Teens*. Grand Rapids, MI: Zondervan, 2006.
2. James Strong, LL.D. S.T.D., *The New Strong's Expanded Dictionary of Bible Words*, (Nashville, TN: Thomas Nelson Publishers, 2001), 1091
3. Beth Moore, *Breaking Free: Making Liberty in Christ a Reality in Life* (Nashville, TN: Lifeway Press, 1999), 150

Section IV Introduction:

1. Dr. Lunde has written an excellent book entitled *Following Jesus, the Servant King*, Zondervan Publishers, 2010. In it he discusses at length the Biblical Theology of Covenantal Discipleship.
2. John F. Walvoord & Roy B. Zuck, eds, *The Bible Knowledge Commentary NT: An Exposition of the Scriptures by Dallas Seminary Faculty* (Colorado Spring, CO, 1983), 642

Chapter 14:

1. Dr. Henry Cloud & Dr. John Townsend, *The Mom Factor* (Grand Rapids, MI: Zondervan, 1996), 152
2. There are many excellent books on forgiveness. One of my favorites is *Forgiving the Unforgivable* by Dr. David Stoop.
3. James Strong, LL.D. S.T.D., *The New Strong's Expanded Dictionary of Bible Words*, (Nashville, TN: Thomas Nelson Publishers, 2001), 1164
4. Ibid, 1002
5. Dr. David Stoop & Dr. James Masteller, *Forgiving Our Parents Forgiving Ourselves: Healing Adult Children of Dysfunctional Families*, (Ventura, CA: Regal), 211
6. Ibid, 169
7. Dr. Henry Cloud & Dr. John Townsend, *The Mom Factor* (Grand Rapids, MI: Zondervan, 1996), 81
8. See also Dennis Rainey with David Boehi, *The Best Gift You Can Ever Give Your Parents* (Little Rock, AR: Family Life Publishing, 2005)
9. Leslie Leyland Fields & Dr. Jill Hubbard, *Forgiving Our Fathers and Mothers* (Nashville, TN: Thomas Nelson Publishers, 2014) I highly recommend reading this book for those who have parents who are estranged or mentally ill.
10. Shakespeare, *The Merchant of Venice*, Act IV: Scene 1

Chapter 16:

1. Don and Jan Frank, *Unclaimed Baggage: Dealing with the Past on Your Way to a Stronger Marriage* (Colorado Springs, CO: Nav Press, 2003), 130-131

Epilogue

1. We found out later that my mother's cancer had aggressively spread causing her death.

BIBLIOGRAPHY

Alcorn, Randy. *The Grace and Truth Paradox: Responding with Christlike Balance*. Portland, OR: Multnomah, 2009.

Arnold, Clinton E., ed. *Zondervan Illustrated Bible Backgrounds Commentary: Acts*. Grand Rapids, MI: 2002.

Bloomfield, Harold H. with Leonard Felder. *Making Peace with Your Parents: The Key to Enriching Your Life and All Your Relationships*. New York: Ballantine Books, 1983.

Bock, Darrell L., ed. *The Bible Knowledge Word Study, Acts-Ephesians*. Colorado Springs, CO: Cook Communications Ministries, 2006.

Darrell L. Bock, *The NIV Application Commentary: Luke*. Grand Rapids, MI: Zondervan, 1996.

Buhler, Rich. *Pain and Pretending: You Can Be Set Free from the Hurts of the Past*. Nashville, TN: Thomas Nelson Publishers, 1988.

Carson, D. A. *The Gospel According to John*. Grand Rapids, MI: William B. Eerdmans Publishing Company, 1991.

Cloud, Henry and John Townsend. *Boundaries: When To Say Yes How to Say No To Take Control of Your Life*. Grand Rapids, MI: Zondervan, 1992.

———. *How People Grow: What the Bible Reveals About Personal Growth*. Grand Rapids, MI: Zondervan, 2001.

———. *The Mom Factor*. Grand Rapids, MI: Zondervan, 1996.

Fields, Leslie Leyland and Jill Hubbard. *Forgiving Our Fathers and Mothers: Finding Freedom from Hurt and Hate*. Nashville, TN: Thomas Nelson Publishers, 2014.

Forward, Susan with Craig Buck. *Toxic Parents: Overcoming Their Hurtful Legacy and Reclaiming Your Life*. New York: Bantam Books, 1989.

Frank, Don and Jan Frank. *Unclaimed Baggage: Dealing with the Past on Your Way to a Stronger Marriage*. Colorado Springs, CO: NavPress, 2003.

Frank, Jan. *Door of Hope: Recognizing and Resolving the Pains of Your Past*. Nashville, TN: Thomas Nelson Publishers, 1995.

Halpern, Howard M. *Cutting Loose: An Adult's Guide to Coming to Terms with Your Parents*. New York: Simon and Schuster, 1990.

Lockyer, Herbert. *All the Women of the Bible*. Grand Rapids, MI: Zondervan, 1988.

Moo, Douglas J. *The Life Application Bible Commentary: Romans*. Grand Rapids, MI: 2000.

Moore, Beth. *Breaking Free: Making Liberty in Christ a Reality in Life*. Nashville, TN: Lifeway Press, 1999.

———. *To Live is Christ* (Nashville, TN: B and H Publishing Group, 2001.

Rainey, Dennis with David Boehi. *The Best Gift You Can Ever Give Your Parents*. Little Rock, AR: Family Life Publishing, 2005.

Sell, Charles. *Unfinished Business: Helping Adult Children Resolve Their Past*. Portland, OR; Multnomah, 1989.

Sichel, Mark. *Healing from Family Rifts: Ten Steps to Finding Peace After Being Cut Off From a Family Member*. New York: McGraw-Hill, 2004.

Stoop, David and James Masteller. *Forgiving Our Parents, Forgiving Ourselves: Healing Adult Children of Dysfunctional Families*. Ventura, CA: Regal, 1991.

Stoop, David. *Forgiving the Unforgivable*. Ventura, CA: Regal, 2005.

Strong, James. *The New Strong's Expanded Dictionary of Bible Words*. Nashville, TN: Thomas Nelson Publishers, 2001.

Townsend, John, *Boundaries with Teens*. GrandTapids, MI: Zondervan, 2006.

Walvoord John F. and Roy B. Zuck, eds. *The Bible Knowledge Commentary NT: An Exposition of the Scriptures by Dallas Seminary Faculty*. Colorado Springs, CO, 1983.

Wilkins, Michael J. *The NIV Application Commentary: Matthew*. Grand Rapids, MI: Zondervan, 2009.

Zodhiates, Spiros, ed. *The Complete Word Study Dictionary NT*. Chattanooga, TN: AMG Publishers, 1992.

ABOUT THE AUTHOR

Jan Frank, LMFT is a licensed marriage, family therapist with more than twenty years of experience counseling individuals, couples, and families from a biblically based perspective. She is a popular speaker at women's events, retreats and professional conferences and the author of *Door of Hope: Recognizing and Resolving the Pains of Your Past* and *A Graceful Waiting*. Jan and her husband, Don, live in California.

CPSIA information can be obtained at www.ICGtesting.com
Printed in the USA
LVOW07s1944291214

420763LV00002B/291/P